MOBILITY TRAINING FOR PEOPLE WITH DISABILITIES

ABOUT THE AUTHOR

After graduating from Brandeis University with a major in psychology, William Goodman earned a master's degree from Boston College in peripatology and then a doctorate from The Florida State University in special education and rehabilitation.

He worked for many years as a mobility instructor with students having a cross-section of disabilities and as a supervisor of other mobility instructors. At The Florida State University, he prepared college seniors to become mobility instructors.

His professional work has included assignments in England, Norway, Sweden, and Germany.

Dr. Goodman has published numerous articles in professional journals, including a widely acclaimed article entitled: "When you meet a blind person."

MOBILITY TRAINING FOR PEOPLE WITH DISABILITIES

Children and Adults with Physical, Mental, Visual and Hearing Impairments Can Learn to Travel

By

WILLIAM GOODMAN, PH.D.

CHARLES C THOMAS • PUBLISHER
Springfield • Illinois • U.S.A.

Published and Distributed Throughout the World by

CHARLES C THOMAS • PUBLISHER
2600 South First Street
Springfield, Illinois 62794-9265

© *1989 by* CHARLES C THOMAS • PUBLISHER

ISBN 0-398-05572-6

Library of Congress Catalog Card Number: 88-36842

With THOMAS BOOKS *careful attention is given to all details of manufacturing
and design. It is the Publisher's desire to present books that are satisfactory as to their
physical qualities and artistic possibilities and appropriate for their particular use.*
THOMAS BOOKS *will be true to those laws of quality that assure a good name
and good will.*

Printed in the United States of America
SC-R-3

Library of Congress Cataloging-in-Publication Data

Goodman, William, 1936–
    Mobility training for people with disabilities : children and
adults with physical, mental, visual, and hearing impairments can
learn to travel / by William Goodman.
        p. cm.
    Includes index.
    ISBN 0-398-05572-6
    1. Handicapped—Travel—United States.   2. Blind—United States—
Orientation and mobility.   3. Rehabilitation—United States—Study
and teaching.   4. Life skills—United States—Study and teaching.
I. Title.
HV 1568.6.G66   1989
362.1'0425—dc19   88-36842
                                                                                          CIP

This book is dedicated to the continuing struggle of people with disabilities to gain or regain independence of movement. Their quiet courage and perseverance, despite countless hardships, rank high among human achievements.

FOREWORD

Mobility Training for People with Disabilities is must reading for all rehabilitation practitioners, therapists, significant others in the life of a disabled person, and for the disabled individual himself. It's must reading because one concludes that mobility is almost as important as breathing, that disabilities of every type have an impact to some degree on the disabled person's mobility, and that the impairment of mobility is a universal handicap no matter what the cause. Mobility impairment is a universal consideration, but the particular disability bears on the mechanics that must be applied in order to overcome the handicap created by impairment to one's mobility.

Dr. Goodman states that: "Combining the fruits of knowledge derived from each separate disability into an intelligible whole creates our most valuable tool for combating mobility problems in whatever form they may appear." And that: "Fear is one of the most common psychological barriers and the one that interferes most often with mobility." And: "It's easier to talk about inaccessible buildings than to face one's inner fears." Throughout his text the reader is helped to understand that mobility training is much more than simply learning mechanics and mastering techniques.

Too often, one hears the words "mobility training" and thinks primarily of persons who are blind, learning to get about with a white cane. But deaf persons, those who must use wheelchairs, those who live with retardation or the uncorrectable results of brain damage due to head injury and other causes, all attain their maximum degree of independence through purposefully directed mobility training. While training may be initiated by properly credentialled individuals, family, friends, and neighbors need not be excluded from the exciting process of assisting a disabled person attain their maximum state of mobility. As the book points out, much of the training has to do with building confidence for the purpose of the disabled person's assuming an appropriate role in society with a maximum degree of comfort and competence.

vii

Finally, *Mobility Training for People with Disabilities* is no slouch when it comes to describing in-depth approaches in respect to the mechanics of assisting people with specific disabilities regarding their mobility handicap. Clear, concise, easy to read detail is given regarding the mechanics of assisting individuals who live with blindness, deafness, paraplegia and quadraplegia, brain injury, stroke, retardation and learning disabilities. This text should be particularly helpful in assisting multiply-handicapped individuals because of the universal approach to mobility training that Dr. Goodman takes.

The reason every rehabilitation practitioner should read this text is that appropriate space will be given to a client's plan once the importance of mobility is understood. Physical therapists, occupational therapists, nursing staff, and other health-related personnel will gain a sense of when mobility instruction is warranted and the degree to which it should be included in the patient's rehabilitation. The significant others in the life of a disabled person will obtain an in-depth understanding of the difficulty their loved one must face in the attainment of his maximum independence regarding a capacity to move. Disabled clients will obtain a detached appreciation of the difficulties they must overcome in order to regain mobility, thereby setting appropriate expectations in respect to the difficult course they must follow.

I hope you will gain as much knowledge and experience, as much excitement as I have about mobility from reading this book. I predict it will become a classic. Dr. William Goodman has made a real contribution to the art of rehabilitation science by defining the importance of mobility.

Paul L. Scher, C.R.C.
Manager, Selective Placement and
Rehabilitation Services
Sears, Roebuck and Company

FOREWORD

In this life, no man makes it on his own. Throughout his life he receives help from family, friends, teachers, colleagues, and even total strangers. He has also received help from long-gone generations for the contributions they made in their attempt to improve the human condition. Therefore, every man is a debtor, and the only way he can pay off this debt is by helping his fellow man.

This debt is especially true for the disabled man: He has received help from doctors, nurses, and a wide variety of therapists in addition to the "traditional" group that includes family and friends. Indeed, the disabled man owes more than his able-bodied brethren.

The disabled man begins to pay his debt by rehabilitating himself with the help of others. While this increases the debt, it enables him to be in a better position to make a greater contribution.

I have spent the last dozen years in the Federal Civil Service helping my fellow man while helping myself. But my rehabilitation would have been impossible and my contributions would have gone for naught had I not been able to transport myself independently to and from many different locations on a regular basis.

During my rehabilitation, I received bits and pieces of what we now call mobility training from a variety of therapists. What they couldn't teach me I picked up from friends, both able-bodied and disabled, or discovered and devised for myself. A book on the subject of mobility training would have been of great assistance to me during my rehabilitation, but none existed, or if it did, it escaped my attention. Such a book could have saved me countless hours in reinventing existing mobility training "wheels" of which I was unaware. A mobility training book could have also saved the time I wasted waiting for others to help transport me when with a little bit of self-taught training I could have transported myself.

This book is not the last word in mobility training; no book can be because the field is constantly being written, rewritten, and revised. Let's just call my contribution to this book one of my many installment payments to my fellow man. It is my sincerest hope that the reader will receive some benefit from this book, thereby relieving me from a portion of my debt while adding to the reader's debt, which I'm sure he'll pay back to his fellow men in his own time and in his own way.

Charles A. Linster
Rehabilitation Services Program Specialist
Rehabilitation Services Administration
U.S. Department of Education
Region V Office
Chicago, Illinois

Mr. Linster's contribution to this book is his own and should not be considered the opinion of the Rehabilitation Services Administration.

FOREWORD

Several years ago, I watched Dr. Goodman's students at The Florida State University as they simulated blind people while walking about the campus and the City of Tallahassee. At that time, I viewed mobility and mobility instruction as a relatively new professional discipline that was concerned only with people with severe visual disabilities. It soon became apparent that mobility training is highly important for people with a variety of handicapping conditions, including people with mental retardation. For that matter, mobility training is significant for us all, and the significance of mobility for all people, especially people with handicaps is a focus of this book.

Dr. Goodman's book is not written for the academician, though there may be much of academic interest. It is not sprinkled with footnotes or citations, but it is a practical book which describes the early and recent history of mobility or peripatology (which literally means traveling on foot). Examples of some of the mobility challenges for people with different handicaps are scattered throughout the book. Hints for overcoming these challenges are contained within the examples.

Certainly, though examples of mobility needs and instruction are given for people with disabilities other than visual, the book still focuses on individuals with visual disabilities. This is understandable considering Dr. Goodman's broad experience in mobility instruction with people with visual disabilities in this and other countries. However, I found, as I read the book, that I frequently speculated that the principles discussed would be applicable to the mobility instructional needs of individuals with whatever disability might be exhibited.

Briefly, as an individual who is an administrator of a state mental retardation program, I liked the book. If readers wish to know what mobility instruction is and is not; if they wish to know of some of the barriers to adequate individual mobility; if they wish to know of individual risks associated with becoming mobile; and if they wish to know of the numerous skills that must be possessed before an individual can become mobile, then I believe such readers will enjoy this book.

James G. Foshee, Ph.D.
Assistant Commissioner,
Tennessee Department of Mental Health
and Mental Retardation

PREFACE

This book grew out of my experience during the past three decades teaching disabled children and adults to travel, as well as training students to become mobility instructors at The Florida State University. Although I have worked primarily with visually impaired people, many of my students were multiply impaired, having such additional disabilities as mental retardation, deafness, and physical impairments. My doctoral dissertation focused on the mobility problems of youngsters who were mentally retarded and those who were physically disabled. While working as a psychologist in Norway, I organized a course for physically disabled adults that focused on their mobility problems.

These experiences convinced me that travel problems are common to most disabled people, more pronounced in some than in others, but always to be found. They lead me to believe that the basic principles used in solving mobility problems for people having one type of disability are applicable to people having dissimilar disabilities. I further believe that the problems associated with getting around can be significantly reduced, sometimes eliminated, through mobility training.

This book is a composite of my experiences, observations, and suggestions about the arduous but rewarding process of learning to travel. It was enriched by countless conversations about mobility with disabled and nondisabled people alike. Whatever its shortcomings, I sincerely hope that this book will help disabled people achieve greater mobility; that it will guide family members and friends as they extend a loving, helping hand; that it will strengthen the efforts of mobility practitioners, classroom teachers, health care providers and administrators; and that it will increase the understanding of students who are preparing to work with disabled people, not only of mobility, but of the nature of living with a disability.

The pronoun "he" is often used when the actual meaning refers to both genders, to avoid the cumbersome repetition of "he or she." The term "disabled person" is often used rather than the more proper but longer phrase "a person with a disability." Rather than alternating between the terms "disabled" and "handicapped," I used the term "disabled" consistently to encompass the overlapping meanings of both terms. I hope that these decisions in writing style do not offend any group or individual.

I gratefully acknowledge the following people for their encouragement to complete this book and for their constructive comments: Dr. Milton Graham (deceased), Leslie Clark, Dr. Richard Umsted, Robert Esposito, Charles Linster, Robert Griffin, James Charlton, Steve Fiffer, Paul Scher, Dr. James Foshee, Paul Tavianni, Charles Schubart, and my wife, Susan.

William Goodman, Ph.D.
Chicago, Illinois

CONTENTS

MOBILITY TRAINING FOR PEOPLE WITH DISABILITIES

Chapter 1

WHAT IS MOBILITY?

Millions of people with disabilities are extremely limited in their ability to go from place to place, even at a time when increased mobility is a hallmark of American society. For many reasons, it is difficult—seemingly impossible at times—for many disabled people to enjoy the ease of mobility taken for granted by those who travel wherever they want without a second thought.

This book sheds light on the widespread problem of personal mobility by focusing on four major themes: (1) How restricted mobility affects the lives of people with disabilities; (2) Specific problems that prevent them from achieving travel patterns consistent with their mobility potential; (3) Constructive ideas about attaining greater independence; and (4) Relevant suggestions that professional workers, as well as family and friends, can use to assist in nurturing mobility competencies.

This book spotlights obstacles—both physical and psychological—which hamper independent travel. It emphasizes both the incapacitating inner barriers, such as fear and anxiety, and external obstacles, such as architectural barriers. It points out practical steps for removing roadblocks from the traveler's path, honing relevant skills, banishing fears, and embracing a positive attitude.

Some questions addressed are: Who is responsible for teaching mobility skills? How can health care workers and teachers—other than mobility specialists—contribute to mobility training? What kind of supportive role can be played by family and friends? How can a disabled person help herself or himself become more mobile? What are the essential ingredients of mobility training? These and other questions are answered as a means of exploring this complex subject and making it comprehensible.

Neither the responsibility for teaching mobility nor the competence to teach it rests solely in the hands of one person or of one professional discipline. Mobility training is carried out by various people who touch the life of a disabled person, by professional workers, as well as by family

3

members and friends. Their contributions may overlap, but each retains a distinct role. Coordination of effort in a unified approach resembles the smooth workings of a team. The focal point is the disabled person himself, who eventually becomes the captain of the mobility training team, the most responsible player.

The people who influence the growth of mobility skills include occupational and physical therapists, classroom and rehabilitation teachers, family members and friends—all those who are eager to play a supportive role, however low-keyed, in the quest for self-reliance and self-respect. Disabled people themselves may discover a fresh perspective as they grapple with the peaks and valleys of reaching their desired destinations.

This book is not a step-by-step manual for mobility training, nor does it aim to transform every reader into a mobility specialist—such a goal would be irresponsible and unrealistic. Rather, this book aims to ensure that the fundamentals of mobility training are not shrouded in mystery, and to increase understanding and effectiveness among those involved with helping disabled people lead satisfying, productive lives.

The information and ideas contained in these pages may serve as a resource for practitioners, as a specialized supplement to their professional training. It also dispels the notion that mobility specialists exclusively have the knowledge to teach every aspect of mobility. Invariably, the most valuable resource for a disabled person is a closely-knit team of informed, caring people—a collaborative effort of professionals, family members, and friends.

It is not feasible to gather into a single curriculum guide all travel skills for every type of disability at every level of development. Nor can a single guide take into account such variations as a student's age, motivation, and personality—not to mention the combined effect of two or more disabilities, or the overall circumstances of the student's life.

What can be done, however, is to construct a conceptual framework, a core curriculum adaptable for helping people with any type of impairment or combination of disabilities, whether young children or elderly men and women. This core curriculum identifies major mobility problems and suggests instructional strategies for reducing them. Workers in various fields can adapt these suggestions to shape appropriate tools for specific students in real situations. Family members and friends can also benefit from these ideas, especially if they are used in conjunction with professional supervision.

DEFINITION OF MOBILITY AND RELATED WORDS

Mobility refers to the diverse set of challenges facing a traveler and to the physical and mental skills required to meet those challenges. Beginning with such seemingly simple tasks as getting out of a hospital bed or crossing a room, the scope of mobility extends to travel in a congested city. It includes such practical skills as finding a restroom, going up and down stairs, using escalators, crossing streets, locating a bus or train stop, shopping in all kinds of stores. It includes planned, purposeful trips as well as leisurely strolls and recreational excursions. Traveling by airplane on business or pleasure trips across the country, or even to a foreign destination, comes under the heading of mobility.

With this diversity in mind, **mobility** can be defined as the act of going from one place to another safely and effectively, on short trips indoors and on long journeys outdoors, making full use of whatever mechanical, technological, or human resources are needed.

In work with visually impaired students, the compound term **orientation and mobility training** is often used to underscore the importance of mental powers, such as maintaining one's bearings in relation to the compass points and to an ever-changing environment, and sticking to a chosen route without getting confused or lost. The word orientation emphasizes an awareness of the travel environment. It means knowing where you are, where you are going, and how to get there. The term orientation and mobility is commonly used in its abbreviated form, O and M. Mobility specialists are often referred to as O and M instructors.

Peripatology is a synonym for O and M. Derived from Latin roots, it literally means the study of traveling on foot. Originally used in 1960, it identified the master's degree program at Boston College which trains mobility instructors for visually impaired people. Graduates of that program are frequently called **Peripatologists**. (As a member of the initial class and one of the first to be employed as a peripatologist, I experienced surprised reactions to this spanking new term, which included puzzled double-takes at the novel sound of the word.) A debate ensued about what to call mobility specialists with graduate degrees, and simpler terms such as mobility instructor won out. But peripatology survives in the vocabulary of some special education and rehabilitation workers, largely because the term conveys a sense of the complexity of this field of study.

Mobility education is most appropriate when referring to teaching mobility skills to school-aged youngsters. This term also includes work with preschoolers and their parents.

The word **travel** often appears interchangeably with the word mobility, to denote going from one place to another, for people with or without disabilities. But travel usually emphasizes movement over a relatively long distance, while mobility encompasses short trips as well as long ones.

Another word in the mobility lexicon is **transportation**. The image conjured up by this word is replete with cars, buses, trains, and airplanes. This umbrella term embraces travel on any type of vehicle—the school bus, subways—but does not suggest the mental and physical skills required to ride those vehicles. Sometimes this word is used as a synonym for mobility. (Webster's dictionary defines transportation as the conveyance from one place to another, especially over long distances. This definition underscores the primary focus on vehicles rather than on travel skills.)

The words **locomotion** and **ambulation** identify specific kinds of mobility, most often in mentally or physically impaired people. Both words emphasize getting about indoors, in a protected environment, such as within a rehabilitation center, school, or residence. Locomotion refers to the most rudimentary movement, such as creeping or crawling. Ambulation denotes walking unassisted. Generally, individuals who can walk unaided are labeled ambulatory, while those who cannot, or depend on a wheelchair, are labeled nonambulatory. Medicaid regulations identify individuals who are unable to walk but can move from place to place with mechanical assistance, such as a wheelchair. (*Webster's Dictionary* defines locomotion simply as the power of moving from one place to another, and ambulation as the act of moving, especially by walking about.)

Gait training is a term used by occupational therapists and physical therapists when teaching a patient who has suffered a stroke, for example, to regain the ability to walk safely without losing balance, perhaps with the aid of braces, crutches, a cane, or a walker. Training aims to strengthen leg muscles, maintain balance, and increase bodily coordination. If the patient is fitted with a prosthesis (artificial limb), gait training focuses on eliminating irregularities of gait caused by walking with such a device.

As you can see, a variety of words are used to label varying aspects of mobility, each word lending a different shade of emphasis and meaning. Selection of a particular term is determined by the kind of disability and by the professional discipline of the user. Becoming aware of similarities and distinctions among these terms will add to your understanding of mobility, when reading about it, discussing it, or assisting someone.

TYPES OF DISABILITIES

What types of disabilities are likely to involve mobility limitations? A realistic answer is that most, if not all disabilities, restrict a person's freedom of movement to some extent, depending on many factors, such as the degree of severity. Heading the list of disabilities which lead to limited mobility are physical, mental, visual, and hearing impairments.

Some people are born with a neurological impairment. Cerebral palsy, for example, is an umbrella term for a group of disabling conditions resulting from central nervous system damage. It is a congenital disability which may cause spasticity, muscular incoordination, a limited range of motion, and speech disturbances. Mothers who contracted rubella (German measles) during the first trimester of pregnancy account for a high incidence of babies born with neurological disorders which adversely affected vision, hearing, and mental development.

Other people become disabled later in life, due to illness, disease, or trauma—in auto accidents, in diving, skiing, or other athletic mishaps—creating irreversible spinal cord or head injuries, blindness, or deafness. Adult-onset disability may also be caused by such conditions as muscular dystrophy, multiple sclerosis, and strokes, to name only a few. Some disabled people are confined to wheelchairs, while others can walk on a limited basis, perhaps with double long-legged steel braces, aluminum crutches, or a walker.

Blind people are arbitrarily considered to be **congenitally blind** if their visual loss began any time before age five, because their mental concepts throughout life would most likely not be based on visual images. Those blinded later in life are referred to as being **adventitiously blind**. A similar distinction is drawn between congenital and adventitious deafness. Those who have no memory of spoken language are considered to be congenitally deaf, while those who remember spoken language are classified as adventitiously deaf. When deafness occurs before the acquisition of language, usually before 3 years of age, the person has no language frame of reference and is considered to have prelingual deafness. The person who becomes deaf after the acquisition of language, usually after the age of 3, has a relatively strong language base and is considered to have postlingual deafness.

One of the leading causes of blindness is glaucoma, which refers to abnormal pressure on the optic nerve. The pressure may reduce peripheral vision and leave central vision essentially intact (tunnel vision). Cataracts, caused by aging, disease, or injury, cloud the lens of the eye and blur vision. Advances in eye surgery, such as ocular implants, reduce the impact of cataracts by correcting much of the blurring. Macular degeneration erodes some or all central vision, but leaves side or peripheral vision unaffected. Other common causes include detached retinas and diabetic retinopathy. Although visual impairment can strike at any age, the majority of blind people are over 60, so it is primarily a problem of old age. A relatively small percentage of people are born with that problem.

In recent years, the term **physically challenged** has become popular as a more positive way to identify people with disabilities. This term emphasizes the extra effort required to lead a satisfying life.

As the longevity revolution continues unabated, with no end in sight, great numbers of people are enjoying greater life expectancy. But, at the same time, many older people are fenced off from desired activities by diminished strength and physical incapacity. Lifelong mobility habits are curtailed as restricted travel becomes an all-too-common fact of life. Someone who drove a car for decades may no longer be able to afford a car, or failing eyesight may jeopardize safe driving, forcing a choice between staying home or using public transportation. Buses and subways may be perceived as fraught with the danger of close contact with crowds of strangers. The incidence of arthritis is high among the elderly. It robs many of their freedom of movement, causing them to become neighborhood-bound or even home-bound.

For every disability, there is a progressive range of severity extending from the mild to the severe. Visual disabilities range from total blindness to legal blindness, a condition which includes considerable functional vision. A person is legally blind if his vision after the best possible correction is 20/200 in the better eye, or if his vision in the better eye subtends an angle of no more than 20 degrees. In the education system, the designation of legal blindness qualifies students for special educational services. Legal blindness among adults makes them eligible for services from agencies serving the blind and certain government benefits, such as an additional deduction on income tax returns.

Low vision, or partial sightedness, refers to the visual range between normal vision and legal blindness, between visual acuity of less than

20/70 and greater than 20/200. It is subnormal vision that cannot be corrected with conventional eyeglasses or contact lenses, yet is not severe enough to meet the standard of legal blindness. The majority of visually impaired people are partially sighted. Age-related vision loss causes 40 percent of elderly people to see blurred faces, fuzzy print, and poorly outlined objects. Less than 10 percent of all visually impaired people are totally blind.

The range of mental retardation extends from those with mild mental deficiencies, people who may function relatively unassisted in society, to the profoundly affected, who must be supervised throughout their lives. A large number of people with varying degrees of mental retardation are born with Down syndrome, which was named after an English physician who first identified the syndrome in 1866. This syndrome is associated with the presence of extra chromosomal material in every cell of the body.

Some people with physical impairments walk with a cane, while others move about only in a wheelchair. Where a person fits into this range of independent mobility determines the nature of his mobility problems, the extent to which he can cope with those problems, and the kind of assistance or training he may need. Hearing impairments range from minute loss to profound deafness. Deafness usually means the inability to learn and understand speech. Hearing impairment is the single most prevalent chronic physical disability in the America, affecting over 13 million people.

Although people with one type of disability differ from those having other disabilities, and individuals having the same disability differ from one another, restricted mobility stands out strikingly as a common concern for people with any type of disability. This book explores the link between all disabilities and personal mobility patterns. It identifies specific causes of limited travel and suggests strategies for widening travel boundaries for people of all ages, from toddlers to the elderly.

The reason for this generic approach is that a great deal can be learned from the distinct challenges posed by each disability and by the way those challenges are met. The body of knowledge and experience associated with each disability can be adapted to people having dissimilar disabilities in a kind of cross-pollination. Combining the fruits of knowledge derived from each separate disability into an intelligible whole creates our most powerful tool for combating mobility problems in whatever form they may appear.

Another advantage is that many people are multiply disabled, having two or more distinct impairments, such as deaf-blindness or the coupling of mental retardation with a physical disability. A noncategorical approach makes it easier to zero in on fundamental mobility problems, without being stymied by the unfamiliar profile of one particular disability. So the whole range of disabling conditions and their connection to mobility habits is the core of this book.

THE VALUE OF MOBILITY

If a disabled person is not mobile at a level near his potential, the effectiveness of all other special education and rehabilitation services is blunted and his quality of life compromised. Achieving a reasonable level of mobility is a high priority goal, directly linked to active participation in life, and to establishing one's place in society.

A milestone is passed by the person who once could not move unaided beyond his own room and then learns to walk unassisted down a nearby corridor, and by a wheelchair-user, once limited to movement on one floor of a building, who is able to travel to a variety of locations. They are expanding, in this small but significant way, both the physical and psychological boundaries of their immediate environment. The drive to be mobile persists as the disabled person battles against shrinking circles of activity. It seems that, by nature, people are compelled to move about, even when circumstances conspire to restrain that drive.

With increased mobility, doors open to places, activities, and events that otherwise would remain tightly shut. It means a better chance to forge and maintain a productive role in society, as an employer, employee or volunteer; a better chance to participate in religious, social, recreational, cultural, and political activities. The world of organized sports programs for people with disabilities might become more enticing, including golfing and skiing for blind people, and racing and basketball for wheelchair users. In so many ways, mobility enhances opportunities to lead a full life and to feel like a whole person.

Progress in mobility has the power to bolster other aspects of personal growth. It bears positively on overall adjustment and on a healthy self-image. It threads its way through many other vital skills connected with independent living. Satisfactory mobility can mean the difference between running errands for one's family or relying on others for most of one's personal needs; between remaining in an institution or functioning in a community-based program; between working or not working; between a job in a sheltered workshop or working in competitive employment; between hope for the future or unalterable despair.

As neighbors and others notice the disabled traveler crossing streets, riding buses or subways, shopping for himself, they develop a sense of respect and admiration, not only for an inspiring display of travel skills, but for the human dignity and irrepressible drive toward independence they represent. Disabled people who move about in public send out positive messages which counter stereotypes of helplessness. They become a more visible part of the community, and at the same time, raise the public's consciousness about the needs and achievements of people with disabilities. These daily ventures into the thick of life highlight the common bond linking all human beings, so that perceived gaps between people with and without disabilities shrink, possibly becoming easier to bridge.

As disabled persons learn to travel independently, their families delight in pride of accomplishment and they welcome their dwindling responsibility to accomodate mobility needs. By easing the burden of dependency, a long stride is taken toward more harmonious relationships and family equilibrium.

Although traveling entails certain risks, there are also weighty risks in remaining homebound or completely dependent on others for everyday needs. There is the risk of feeling dehumanized, of losing one's sense of dignity, of being isolated from neighbors and disconnected from one's community. Taking risks is a normal part of life, an essential nutrient for human growth. When the opportunity to take reasonable risks is denied, stagnation replaces growth, and the life-renewing stimulus of fresh experiences dangles frustratingly out of reach.

There appears to be a direct link between restricted mobility and the spread of psychological stress. During the past two decades, countless articles in the media have trumpeted the connection between exercise and the elevation of mood, between walking or running and a sense of well-being. During exercise the body releases mood-elevating chemicals called endorphins, which help to wipe away worries. Physical activity works as a "stress-buster," relieving anxiety and easing depression. It appears to promote physical health by strengthening heart muscles and lowering blood pressure. It seems to tranquilize emotions and boost mental health. Being able to go places just for fun is good medicine.

Although the link between physical exercise and mental health has been firmly established for average people, its implications have special relevance for those who are mobility-limited. Incorporating travel into one's daily routine combats the downside of disability. The arthritic is encouraged to move every joint in his body; the wheelchair-user is advised to exercise the upper part of his body by pushing the wheels, rather than being pushed by someone else. Even some people who suffer from backaches are urged to exercise. Some people with disabilities participate in organized sports activities, such as golfing and skiing for blind people and basketball and racing for people in wheelchairs, making use of all the faculties at their command. Incredibly, a young man rolled around the world in his wheelchair, and a game amputee "walked" across Canada by rocking forward on his hands.

Using one's abilities to the fullest becomes the battle cry. Muscles wasted from inaction or deterioration of the body parts from disuse cannot exert a positive influence on anyone's mental outlook. Social isolation and dependency aggravate a sense of loneliness, of languishing without purpose or direction, which in turn leads to hopelessness and feelings of despair.

If a disabled person cannot surmount mobility barriers, how can he or she aspire to higher goals such as cultivating a gratifying social life or becoming a productive member of society? Clearly, travel skills by themselves will not resolve all of life's problems, but they stand near the center of any serious effort to come to grips with them. For this reason, the improvement of travel habits deserves close attention from disabled people and from those seriously concerned about their betterment.

Some disabled people succeed with a self-directed program of mobility training. Others lean on friends and family to acquire the fundamentals of travel. Some disabled people require assistance from a mobility specialist or other interested professional. Still others succeed by taking advantage of a combination of these options.

No matter how comprehensive mobility training is, it never covers everything the traveler needs to know. Learning to travel is a lifelong process. Even those who have been trained must continue to learn through their own trial-and-error experiences. It cannot be assumed that all disabled people learn to travel independently by teaching themselves, nor that all disabled people require the services of a mobility specialist.

ILLUSTRATIVE EXAMPLES

The following fictitious examples illustrate how disabled people resemble and differ from one another as they assert themselves toward greater independence. Consider the story of Jack Parsons, 19, paralyzed from the neck down due to an accident while competing as a gymnast during his freshman year at a midwestern college. In the middle of a forward flip, his hands slipped as he reached for the uneven parallel bar and he slammed into the mat, head first. As he lay there staring at the ceiling, he knew that his neck was broken but he clung to the hope that somehow it could be fixed. It couldn't.

He spent the first eight months after the accident recuperating from the physical and psychological effects of trauma, most of that time in a hospital and then a rehabilitation center. A physician told him that technically he was a quadriplegic, that he could not expect to regain any practical use of his legs, although some strength remained in his arms. Depression robbed him of the energy needed to pull himself together. He grieved for the loss of functioning in his limbs. At times he refused to budge from his bed unless prodded by a watchful nurse.

A devoted younger brother visited often, spinning the best pep talks he could muster to pry Jack out of his doldrums. Jack later recalled that these persistent, but seemingly futile ministerings, sparked his eventual decision to snap out of it and get on with his life. Also, Jack noticed that other patients with similar disabilities were trying their best to move ahead in the hallways and in therapy sessions.

Gradually, as an inner urge grew to recapture a piece of his former independence, Jack stopped feeling sorry for himself. He resolved to shape up and learn to get around on his own. Though it meant feeling like a rank beginner, he was now ready to start all over again. He refused to accept the physician's pronouncement that there could be no improvement. He set out to prove that the physician's prognosis was wrong. Jack latched onto the hope that hard, steady effort would one day make him mobile again. He would employ the kind of sweat and discipline that had made him a first-rate gymnast. He would compensate for what he lacked in leg power by building upper body strength and by using his brains to guide his resurgence. As his dormant competitive spirit rose again, he said to himself with determination, "I'll give it my best shot."

During his stay in the rehabilitation center, a physical therapist and an occupational therapist, working as a team, prescribed the type and size of wheelchair best suited for his needs. They taught Jack to use the chair effectively. He learned to transfer himself from bed to wheelchair, to roll into an elevator quickly before the doors closed, to cope with bumps on the sidewalk, and to lift his chair in and out of a car. Under their supervision, he built up his shoulder and upper body strength, which helped him cope with the physical demands of controlling his chair under all conditions.

Other staff members influenced the progress of his rehabilitation. He requested permission to practice getting in and out of a taxicab, a dry run for real trips later. The physical therapist declined his request, saying that he wasn't ready. When the psychologist heard about it, she interceded. She said Jack must be given the opportunity because the timing was crucial to his emotional recovery. The psychologist's decision prevailed. Jack practiced the transfer into a cab and felt hopeful about his prospects for getting around unassisted. For the first time in a long while, he felt elated.

Along with his progress were inevitable setbacks. At times he felt as despondent as just after his accident. He presented his doctor with a list of problems, such as the difficulty of getting his toileting under control, and asked what he could do about them. The doctor, well aware of Jack's circumstances and his hard-won progress, looked him squarely in the eye and said with a mixture of firmness and compassion, "This is your disability. What are you going to do about these problems?"

Some of the practical problems he faced were climbing the steps in front of a friend's house, wrestling his chair through a narrow opening in a men's room and using public transportation. Unhappily, Jack discovered that city buses were not equipped to accommodate wheelchairs, and architectural barriers usually placed subway stations out of bounds. Faced with these unwelcome facts of his new life, Jack enrolled in a driver education program at the rehabilitation center and looked forward to the day when he could drive his own hand-controlled car.

With experience, Jack paid less attention to the inevitable stares of the passing public—stares of curiosity and pity. As his sensitivity diminished, he concentrated more on honing the skills he needed to get around. At the same time, he couldn't help feeling proud about the way he whizzed around in his chair. He also enjoyed exercising his upper body and rebuilding his physical strength. Jack came to realize that the wheelchair was not a tragedy, but rather a passport to his new-found freedom. His needs and drives were still there, but he was rechanneling them. Now he felt ready—eager, in fact—to resume his college career.

Back at college, Jack discovered that the campus was barrier-free, complete with ramps and elevators. Either he had not noticed these conveniences before or substantial progress had been made during his absence to comply with federal standards. He appreciated the technical assistance and sincere encouragement provided by the advisor for disabled students, who was always there to run interference whenever problems accumulated.

Jack became acquainted with other disabled students and valued their comaraderie. They were go-getters and fiercely independent. Within this group there was a stigma against anyone who could not get around on his own. This attitude served to spur his own aspirations in mobility. He learned from his friends, but he also competed with them. If they could make it through college, so could he. It felt good to set his sights high and on long-range goals, like earning his college degree and then finding a suitable job.

A counselor from the state Office of Vocational Rehabilitation visited Jack. After determining that he was eligible, the counselor provided funds to defray the cost of his education, including the cost of his special needs. Jack completed his bachelor's degree and went on to earn a master's degree in rehabilitation, again with the help of state funds.

He landed a job with the Rehabilitation Services Administration, a federal agency that oversees programs for disabled people. He married and eventually adopted two children. Jack commutes in his specially-equipped car from his home in the suburbs to his downtown office. He felt lucky to find a parking space he could rent by the month just a half block from his office. On one business trip, he flew to Los Angeles for a meeting. The trip was not problem-free, but he was pleased with his ability to solve each problem as it arose.

Jack serves on a number of committees concerned with improving accessibility for disabled people. As he moves about in public, he holds his head high and feels gratified to serve as an outstanding example of what people with disabilities can achieve. He always takes time to talk to people who are interested—especially youngsters. His life is not easy, but Jack is productive and fulfilled. He feels good about himself!

Now picture another person with a completely different disability in other circumstances. Estelle Langdon is a totally blind woman whose vision began to deteriorate a few years ago due to detached retinas. She was terrified by the prospect of losing her sight, but forced herself to accept the inevitable outcome. She is a strong-willed person who worked hard all her life to attain her goals. Afraid that her sense of identity would be altered by blindness, she fought against the feeling of being swamped by the undercurrents of her disability. She worried that people would no longer relate to her as they had in the past.

A widow for several years, she managed to keep her daily routines intact by taking cabs and accepting rides from her many friends, who were a great source of comfort and support. But she soon realized that this arrangement was not practical on a long-term basis.

After experiencing bouts of despondency and at the urging of her physician, Estelle enrolled in a rehabilitation program at a private agency for the blind, where she received a number of useful services, including mobility training. She was informed about guide dogs and about a nearby guide dog school, but since she didn't like having to care for a dog or remaining in close quarters with it, she chose the long aluminum cane as her best travel tool.

At first Estelle was embarrassed about walking in public with a white cane. It created an image in her mind that clashed with her self-reliant nature. But as mobility training progressed, she grew to appreciate the cane's value. She worked diligently for months to master basic travel skills, including cane techniques, crossing streets, and using public transportation. She put her newly-acquired competencies to good use when she resumed her career as a fundraiser for a nonprofit agency. With practice she improved her ability to thread a path through fast-moving crowds, without tripping people or injuring herself, and could cross intersections jammed with traffic. Her biggest fear continues to be traveling alone at night because of the danger of being mugged. As a safety measure, she never ventures out alone after dark.

Although Estelle travels independently, she seeks help when traveling in unfamiliar parts of the city, when crossing wide streets, or when passing through a hazardous stretch, such as a construction site that unexpectedly appears on an otherwise familiar route. She knows how and when to ask for help, but she is tactful about declining unsolicited help when it is unneeded or unwanted. Always courteous, she thanks people for their assistance and holds up her end of casual conversations.

Estelle is justifiably proud of her hard-earned ability to move about on her own. Her pride is bolstered by the admiration she senses from others who observe her poise and fortitude, even when she occasionally bumps into people or unexpected obstacles. She knows that some onlookers shake their heads in amazement at the sight of her sailing smoothly through crowds.

At first, this shower of attention bothered Estelle and aggravated her feelings of tension and self-consciousness. It felt like an invasion of her privacy. But she grew to understand other people's reactions for what they are: a blend of surprise, an instinctive desire to help, a tip of the hat to a dramatic human accomplishment, and an uneasy realization that blindness could strike anyone.

Harold Dawson is severely retarded due to a brain injury suffered at birth. He is 14 years old and has lived for the past five years in a state institution for people with developmental disabilities. Although he is physically vigorous, his freedom of movement within the institution is strictly limited. He is forbidden to walk alone beyond a nearby recreation area. This tight leash is imposed by staff members who believe Harold would wander off and get lost unless he is closely supervised.

His uncle sometimes visits on Sundays and walks with him. These visits are a real treat for Harold, for the companionship they provide and for the chance to experience other parts of the grounds, occasionally including places of interest beyond the grounds.

Harold's restrictions are required by administrative policy, which is often more concerned with protecting residents from injury than accepting the inevitable risks of developing mobility skills. No staff member was assigned the responsibility of teaching him mobility skills. No one knew whether Harold was capable of learning to walk around the grounds alone because no one had tried to teach him. He never had the chance to demonstrate his capabilities, so his potential for mobility remained unexplored.

On a promising note, the administration of the institution is in the midst of an all-out drive to earn accreditation from a federal agency. Establishing mobility training throughout the institution is an important step toward that goal. The new program would include a review of all rules and regulations governing independent trips by residents, both on and off the grounds.

Harold is being considered for placement in a community-based residential program, a kind of half-way house for people with developmental disabilities. He would live in a group home with round-the-clock supervision, and would enjoy greater freedom to experience life in the community. His mobility would be given a higher priority, and his chances for a brighter future would be enhanced.

Margaret Domus, 18, is classified as trainable mentally retarded and legally blind. A ward of the state, Margaret lives with elderly foster parents who speak Spanish but little English. She attends a special school for retarded students in the Chicago Public Schools.

Margaret is a hard worker who tries earnestly to do her best at whatever she attempts. She is always willing to persevere at any task assigned to her and takes pride in maintaining a neat appearance. She is motivated to use her abilities to the utmost. Margaret wears corrective glasses and makes good use of her residual vision. Eager to feel grown up, it galls her to continue riding the school bus, which she is required to take even though she lives only 20 minutes from the school.

A full-time mobility instructor is assigned to her school. The instructor trains students who are mentally retarded to travel independently on public transportation between home, school, and work sites, where students are placed for vocational experiences. The instructor skipped over Margaret, however, because he had no training or experience in working with visually impaired students. He felt he could not responsibly teach her.

A mobility instructor who specialized in training blind students began to work one afternoon a week at the school and chose Margaret as his first student. He talked with Margaret to get an idea of her expectations about travel, her motivation, and past travel experiences. He quickly discovered she was highly motivated and an excellent candidate for mobility training. The instructor spoke with her foster mother, through an interpreter, and found that she was uneasy about Margaret traveling alone on city buses. She did not feel that Margaret had the ability to do so safely and had little confidence in her capacity to learn. Reluctantly, the foster mother granted permission for training to begin, but remained frightened by the idea.

Training focused on two major problems: riding two buses using a transfer and crossing busy streets controlled by traffic lights near the bus stops. Margaret learned the cost of each bus trip, with and without a transfer, the location of the bus stops, and how to ask the driver to call out the name of the street where she wanted to get off. But the instructor advised her to spot landmarks along the way that would indicate when her stop was approaching, because the driver could not always be relied on to remember her street. The driver might become distracted by the traffic, other passengers, or he could simply forget.

Margaret was not in the habit of scanning the traffic before crossing streets or while walking through an intersection. She had to learn the discipline of looking both ways before stepping off the curb and of listening to the start-up of the traffic moving parallel to her before crossing streets. In her eagerness to impress the instructor with her ability, she tended to rush while crossing, speeding across the intersection even at unsafe times. Correcting this error required patient repetition. She crossed the same streets repeatedly, as the instructor encouraged her with timely, relaxed feedback. His message finally hit home when Margaret realized that, unless she consistently crossed the streets carefully and observed all safety rules, she would not be granted permission to travel alone.

She listened intently to everything the instructor told her, earnestly giving her best effort. It was important for Margaret to accomplish her goal. On one trip, she inadvertently tore her transfer and the driver of the second bus would not accept it. Embarrassed by this slip-up, she apologized to the instructor and vowed never to let it happen again. On the next lesson, just before boarding the second bus, Margaret held the transfer right in front of the instructor's face and said with a big smile: "See, it's not ripped!"

The instructor coached her about appropriate social behavior, because her independent trips on the bus would increase her contact with strangers. "What would you do if a man approached you and started asking personal questions or giving you small gifts?" "How would you call for help if you needed it?" She was quizzed in this way until her answers were consistently satisfactory—one more important detail in preparing for her solo bus trips.

After months of mobility lessons in all kinds of weather, the mobility instructor felt that she was ready to make the trip alone. The school social worker, fully supportive of Margaret's venture, explained to her foster parents that real progress had been made, and that it was important for her to be given their approval to travel alone to school. Reluctantly, permission was granted, and Margaret finally got the green light.

After completing her first solo trip, she beamed with joy at her long-awaited personal triumph, which clearly boosted her self-confidence. Her friends at school, aware of her achievement and eager to match it with their own, viewed her with a new level of respect and admiration. She began to take even more care of her appearance and walked with a happy bounce. Her new status as an independent traveler opened up the possibility of working as an apprentice at a facility off the school grounds and improved her chances of getting a job after graduation. No other single accomplishment in her school career yielded as much personal satisfaction as riding that city bus all by herself.

The people in these examples differ from one another in many respects, but they all underscore a common theme. Mobility is a vital, never-ending need for people of all ages having a variety of disabilities. The examples suggest that the quest for independence is a long-term struggle requiring determination, courage, and a positive attitude, along with the cultivation of practical travel skills.

Chapter 2

HISTORICAL NOTES

Here are some historical highlights and background information about the development of mobility training in the United States, beginning with efforts to help people with visual impairments.

PEOPLE WITH VISUAL IMPAIRMENTS

Scenes in the Bible depict blind people walking with the aid of a stick or a staff. This is an ancient image rooted deeply in the collective consciousness of mankind. Until the mid-nineteenth century, blind people (as well as other groups of disabled people) were cared for by charitable groups, primarily religious organizations, in isolated settings long distances from population centers.

Residential schools for the blind were established before special schools for any other disability group. During the 1830s, residential schools for the blind, sponsored by private sources, opened for the first time in Boston, New York, and Philadelphia. Subsequently, most states established publicly-supported residential schools where, until the mid twentieth century, most visually impaired students were educated. These schools remained separate from the rest of society and emphasized adjustment to a blind subculture, rather than integration into the sighted community.

Limited mobility did not manifest itself as a problem because blind people tended to circulate within narrow boundaries. The idea that disabled people could become independent, that they could be responsible for their own safety while traveling, that they should be accorded full civil rights, that they should secure employment without discrimination, that they should have equal access to public buildings and transportation—these ideas, which today are widely accepted, attracted only sporadic attention at that time. More than a century would pass before public opinion and court decisions gave people with disabilities status as full-fledged citizens.

As the practice of segregation continued into the twentieth century, parents began to challenge a system that separated them from their children in the name of "Education." They spearheaded a national movement to establish educational programs within local school systems, so their children could live at home—not only for the sake of preserving family bonds, but as a more practical way to prepare for living in a sighted world.

In the 1960s and 1970s, the term **integration** became a watchword in special education, paralleling its increasing use in the civil rights movement. The rallying cry behind this term was that, whenever possible, disabled students should be educated alongside their nondisabled peers in local schools, not in distant residential schools. Today, the equivalent term most generally favored is **mainstreaming**. As these trends sink deeper roots into American school systems, more nondisabled students are educated side by side with disabled students in regular classrooms, creating untold numbers of friendships and unprecedented levels of awareness and acceptance.

The culmination of the mainstream movement, which was bolstered by the contributions of many educators, materialized in landmark legislation, PL 94-142, The Education for All Handicapped Children Act of 1975. This federal law mandated that disabled children must be educated in the least restrictive environment. Students enrolled in a residential school, who are capable enough, should be transferred to a neighborhood school. Students being educated in segregated classrooms or in special resource rooms in public school should receive instruction as often as possible in regular classes, side by side with nondisabled students. This law also mandated that an Individual Education Plan (IEP) must be written for each disabled student at an annual meeting attended by teachers, parents, and specialists. The IEP prescribed an educational plan, based on individual needs, that the school was legally bound to implement. Mobility training was often targeted on the IEP as a vital educational service.

Thousands of premature babies were blinded by overdoses of oxygen in hospital incubators during the 1940s and 50s; this eye disorder is known as retrolental fibroplasia (RLF). The number of babies blinded by this inadvertent error continued to rise until medical research identified excessive oxygen in the incubators as the elusive culprit. The rubella epidemics which swept across America during the 1960s also resulted in the birth of thousands of blind babies.

These developments increased the need for mobility training programs in schools and community agencies. As a natural response to this emerging need, mobility programs began to spring up in both residential and public schools. The Perkins School for the Blind, for example, was one of the first residential schools to hire a peripatologist as early as 1962. With mainstreaming, and mobility training, visually impaired children were stepping forward.

As these waves of blind children passed through the school systems, pioneering mobility programs adapted techniques originally devised for blinded veterans and shaped them to suit the travel needs and capabilities of youngsters who were visually impaired. During the 1960s, the federal government played a major role in establishing mobility programs by providing seed money as an enticement for schools to begin thinking about channeling their own funds to support mobility training. The Office of Vocational Rehabilitation, which is now called the Rehabilitation Services Administration (RSA), funded an innovative mobility project for children in Detroit Public Schools, a project coordinated by the Greater Detroit Society for the Blind. RSA funded a similar program in Chicago Catholic Schools.

For several years I supervised the project in Detroit, working for a private agency but teaching blind children in public schools. It was exciting to work in this pioneering project because teaching youngsters to travel was uncharted territory, and all of us involved with the program had to learn as we went along.

In the early 1960s, the idea of working with blind children met with considerable skepticism from those who believed that it was not safe for blind people to travel alone before high school graduation, or at least until their first year of secondary school. But it was soon realized that the earlier a blind child learned the basics of mobility, the better were his chances of eventually mastering travel skills. The sooner the habit of independence became ingrained, the better were his chances of maturing into a contributing citizen.

Today, mobility programs are a firmly established part of the curriculum in both residential and local schools. These programs enjoy the grateful and enthusiastic support of parents, teachers, and administrators. In a real sense, training youngsters to travel has become the new frontier of mobility, stimulating some of the most innovative developments in this young field, such as parent involvement and concept development.

In January 1929, the first American guide dog school, The Seeing Eye, was established by Dorothy Harrison Eustis in Nashville, Tennessee. In June of that year The Seeing Eye moved to its present location in Morristown, New Jersey. It remains one of the most prominent and well-endowed schools of its kind, serving as a model for the other six guide dog schools presently operating in America. Although several breeds of dogs, such as Doberman pinschers and retrievers, have been trained as guide dogs, German shepherds are still the most widely used.

Electronic aids, with names like Mowat Sensor, Pathsounder, and Sonicguide, have captured a small but persistent foothold among blind travelers. They can be used in conjunction with a cane or guide dog, or they can be used alone. One hand-held device operates on the principle of radar: When its ultrasonic waves strike an object, they activate varying sound signals, indicating the approximate size of the object and its distance from the traveler. A laser cane also operates on the radar principle, but employs laser beams rather than ultrasonic waves. It can "see" curbs and stairs and even overhangs, such as awnings, and warn the traveler of impending danger. Some devices are used less as a travel tool and more as a means of exploring the environment, of detecting information about relatively distant objects.

Of all the travel modes used by blind travelers—canes, guide dogs, human guides—none attracts more publicity than these modern devices. Newspaper articles herald "James Bond" devices that spell the end of travel problems for blind people, a misleading exaggeration that plays on America's growing fascination with technological wonders.

In practice, however, relatively few blind people rely on electronic travel aids. Since partially sighted people have little need for them, the remaining pool of potential users—totally or near totally blind people—represents a miniscule market. The majority of totally blind people are elderly and have no interest in learning to travel with these devices. But the small number of people who are trained to use an electronic travel aid, and who incorporate it into their travel routines, give the device high marks. While electronic travel aids remain expensive and some are still experimental, engineers of assistive technology continue to debug them and reduce their cost.

The first city ordinance to protect blind pedestrians when crossing streets was passed in Peoria, Illinois on October 15, 1930, initiated by the Central Lions Club. It worked so well in Peoria that similar white cane traffic laws are now on the books in most states. These laws specify that any blind person carrying a clearly visible white cane or accompanied by a guide dog has the right of way while crossing a street.

While wars produced unprecedented numbers of disabled veterans, they also provided the catalyst for significant advances in rehabilitation. During the later stages of World War II, rehabilitation programs for the swelling numbers of blinded veterans were established in Avon, Connecticut and Valley Forge Army Hospital in Pennsylvania. These early efforts evolved into a full-scale, long-term rehabilitation program at Hines Veterans Administration Hospital outside of Chicago, where quality mobility training continues to be offered.

A young army sergeant at the Valley Forge Hospital, Richard Hoover, who went on to become an ophthalmologist, devised effective techniques for using the long cane to protect blind travelers from obstacles in their paths. These techniques, originally used with blinded veterans, remain the fundamental tools of mobility training today, even in educating blind youngsters to travel.

Vocational rehabilitation provided additional impetus to mobility training. This federal program assists people with disabilities to enter or continue in the work force, helping them become tax-paying citizens rather than welfare recipients. Some states have a separate bureau for the blind, while in other states, vocational services for the blind are included within a general agency serving disabled people.

Mobility training was found to be a boon for people who were otherwise employable, but simply could not solve the problem of getting to work on their own. The federal government, realizing the direct connection between mobility and work, awarded grants to selected agencies serving blind people to enable them to hire mobility instructors. Other agencies simply allocated some of their own funds for this purpose. The growth of mobility programs was reinforced by active consumer groups which applauded the trend toward increased mobility training.

Since 1960, the scope of mobility training has widened as agencies and schools observed the vital benefits that students derived from it. The focus of mobility training shifted from totally blind people to include those with low vision; from young and middle-aged adults to include congenitally blind children as well as visually-impaired older people; and from people whose only disability is blindness to those with additional disabilities, such as retardation and deafness. Mobility instructors increasingly spend time helping students with sensory training, concept development and techniques of daily living.

Father Thomas Carroll, a lifelong advocate of professional services for blinded adults, ministered to the needs of blinded veterans. Subsequently, he became director of a rehabilitation center for blinded adults in Newton, Massachusetts, now called the Carroll Center for the Blind. He was instrumental in convincing officials in the federal Office of Vocational Rehabilitation that mobility training was so vital to the rehabilitation of blind adults that instructors should be professionally prepared in university programs.

In 1960, the federal government started funding programs to train mobility instructors at the master's degree level, first at Boston College and a year later at Western Michigan University. In 1966, also with federal support, the first program to train instructors who were college seniors started at The Florida State University. It was the first time that undergraduates had the opportunity to prepare for this specialized discipline.

As the first instructor for the program in Tallahassee, Florida, I experienced firsthand the controversy surrounding this initial effort to train undergraduates. This innovative endeavor was generally viewed in the mobility field as clashing with the recently established standard of the master's degree. At that time, many professionals in the mobility field disapproved this change of approach, believing it would jeopardize the quality of mobility instruction.

Now, instructors are educated in 11 graduate programs and 3 undergraduate programs, with general acceptance by the mobility profession of both levels of training. Some universities offer dual preparation—in mobility training and classroom teaching of the visually impaired—so graduates can offer both skills to their students, or have a choice between the two professional directions. Many university programs that prepare classroom teachers for the blind require their students to take a course in mobility training, so students can better understand the mobility process and assist blind youngsters in learning basic mobility techniques.

The federal government funded a master's degree program at the University of Wisconsin during the late 1970s to train mobility instructors who were qualified to work with people having any type of disability. This innovative program was discontinued after a few years, partly because of an entrenched tradition that insists on training professional workers for one disability group, rather than equipping them with a generic skill which can be applied to people having different disabilities.

During the past 30 years, mobility training has matured into a vital and expanding profession, taking its place among other essential services for blind people, such as the teaching of braille. As awareness about the undeniable value of mobility spread across the country, in private and public agencies, in schools and rehabilitation centers, the demand for qualified instructors outstripped the supply. This shortage is partly due to a substantial turnover in mobility personnel. Experienced instructors often transfer to other positions within the blindness field or move on to other fields.

Today, the mobility profession is still grappling with a host of unresolved issues. Some agencies serving blind people, exasperated by the chronic shortage of mobility personnel, have taken the matter into their own hands, setting up classes within their agencies to train their own mobility instructors through apprenticeship programs. These agencies have the advantage of handpicking students, perhaps from among existing staff, and paying them lower, more affordable salaries, compared to instructors with master's degrees.

In-service training has stirred a controversy because it does not comply with standards set by the university programs or by the certification requirements established by the Association for Education and Rehabilitation of the Blind and Visually Impaired (AER). This issue continues to be vigorously debated within the mobility profession and within agencies serving visually impaired people. Although the mobility profession has remained skeptical of the quality of agency-trained instructors, and has discouraged the growth of such programs, it is beginning to acknowledge that some kind of compromise must be reached in order to alleviate the chronic shortage of mobility personnel. The mobility certification committee of AER is in the process of working out details for certifying instructors trained under the supervision of certified instructors.

Another controversial issue is: Should visually impaired people be admitted into university training programs and become eligible for AER certification? Ever since university programs started in 1960, no visually impaired students have been admitted, largely because conventional wisdom held that a mobility instructor with less than normal vision could not adequately supervise his students, especially at potentially dangerous places such as busy intersections.

Some visually impaired people, contending that the admission policy to university programs and the AER certification requirements are discriminatory, have challenged them in court. They argue that the requirement of normal or near normal vision deprives them of the opportunity to teach mobility, since most positions are open only to those holding a valid AER certificate.

An exception to this requirement is the State of Iowa, where an AER certificate is not a prerequisite for employment. Many of the mobility instructors in Iowa are visually impaired and some of them double in other capacities, such as in rehabilitation teaching.

Prior to 1960, it was primarily partially sighted and totally blind people who taught mobility in schools and agencies throughout the country. They were considered to be experts in mobility because they possessed personal experience traveling with limited or no eyesight. Now they are wading through legal channels to reclaim their right to teach mobility.

PEOPLE WITH PHYSICAL IMPAIRMENTS

A significant year for the physically impaired traveler was 1933, when a relatively lightweight wheelchair that could be folded for easy storage (in a car, for example) was patented by Everest & Jennings. During the last few decades, motorized wheelchairs and carts, powered by electric batteries, have become popular, adding a valuable mobility option— especially for those unable to engage their upper body strength. The number of options available for wheelchair-mobile people continues to grow.

Among the casualties of World War II were thousands of veterans with irreversible spinal cord and head injuries, many of whom survived their wounds thanks to the use of antibiotics and other medical advances. As veterans returned to their hometowns, public awareness grew regarding the human side of living with a disability. This awareness was sharpened by several popular movies depicting the drama of veterans in wheelchairs, rebuilding their lives, forging a place for themselves in their communities.

One Academy Award winning film by Stanley Kramer, "The Men," starred Marlon Brando in his first film, a movie in which many of the extras were spinal cord injured vets in real life. Another film, "The Best Years of Our Lives," won several oscars: Best Picture of 1946; Best Actor, Frederick March; and Best Supporting Actor, Harold Russell, who is a double-amputee.

As the sheer number of physically disabled people mounted, in part due to the increasing incidence of traffic accidents and the epidemic of poliomyelitis, so did concern about barriers that impede access to buildings and public transportation. During the 1970s, advocacy groups composed primarily of disabled people demanded a barrier-free environment with equal access for all. Willing to settle for nothing less than their full civil rights, coalitions of disabled citizens filed lawsuits, demonstrated, and staged sit-ins in front of public transportation offices and inaccessible buildings, capturing local and sometimes national headlines.

The disability rights movement reached a highwater mark in 1968 with passage of the Architectural Barriers Act, in which Congress directed the federal government to prescribe a national standard for accessibility. This Act mandated that recipients of financial assistance from the federal government may not discriminate against disabled individuals, that most buildings and facilities constructed, renovated, or maintained with federal funds must be accessible and usable by disabled people.

Missing from that act was an enforcement mechanism, a shortcoming which was remedied by another significant milestone, Section 504 of the Rehabilitation Act of 1973. Section 504 established the Architectural and Transportation Barriers Compliance Board, whose main function is to enforce the standards prescribed under the Architectural Barriers Act of 1968.

An organization called the Center for Independent Living gained momentum during the 1970s by providing services to disabled people, including counseling, wheelchair repair, and transportation. Funded by federal, state, and private grants, these centers are staffed largely by disabled people and feature a peer support system. Although the first center originated in Berkeley, California, similar centers with the same name have appeared around the country. This well-organized movement creates alternatives to custodial care.

Despite substantial progress, concerned consumers continue to demonstrate and challenge inequitable practices in court. Their cherished goal of equal access in a barrier-free society will not be abandoned until all structural, transportation, and communicative barriers are eliminated. This relentless campaign points toward the need for a national transportation policy to render mass transit systems accessible to all citizens at a reasonable cost.

The Voting Accessibility for the Elderly and Handicapped Act of 1984 mandates that all polling places must be accessible to people with disabilities. It also provides that aides should be available to help those who cannot mark their ballots unassisted. Ramps must be available at entrances to polling sites. For those who cannot get out of a car to enter the polling site, a portable voting machine can be brought to curbside, as long as it is no further than 50 feet from the polling site.

PEOPLE WITH MENTAL RETARDATION

Attitudes toward and expectations for people with mental retardation have changed significantly over the past 20 years. The needs of retarded people were generously addressed during the Kennedy Administration, partly because President Kennedy, whose sister is retarded, sustained a lively interest in improving services. Deinstitutionalization became a major refrain in the reform movement of the 1960s and 70s. Parent groups lobbied effectively for more programs and services for their youngsters in their own communities, rather than having them spend their entire lives in a distant institution. More and more children with Down syndrome, for example, who had routinely been institutionalized in the past, were living at home.

Transportation emerged as a crucial issue as more community-based programs opened their doors. Since parents could not accompany their disabled daughter or son every day, and agencies could not afford to subsidize all transportation costs, the importance of mobility training became apparent to administrators of those programs.

The major impetus behind the growth of mobility training programs was to enable retarded adults beyond school age to travel independently to workshops and activity programs, to community functions, to shopping, and to other events. Typically, a private agency serving retarded adults, such as the Association for Retarded Citizens, provided on-the-job training for interested staff members who then became the agency's mobility specialists. The training programs for instructors of retarded students borrowed from the mobility expertise developed among instructors for visually impaired students. At present, no programs exist in universities to educate mobility instructors for people who are retarded, largely because mobility training for that disability group has not yet been assigned the priority that it has achieved for visually impaired people.

PEOPLE WITH HEARING IMPAIRMENTS

As their numbers grow, hearing impaired people have benefited from a heightened awareness of their communication needs. Section 504 of the Rehabilitation Act of 1973 mandates that any organization which receives federal funds must provide interpreter services to ensure equal access for deaf persons.

Many TV programs are closed-captioned so that people with hearing impairments can read the text. Selected performances of theatrical productions in large cities, such as New York and Chicago, feature interpreters standing at one side of the stage so deaf people can follow the dialogue and watch the dramatic action at the same time.

Many churches and synagogues have added a special amplification system for hard of hearing people. By plugging a small listening device— similar to a hearing aid—into their ear, the entire religious service becomes audible. Most of the congregants at Temple Bene Shalom in Skokie, Illinois, are deaf, so the Rabbi signs simultaneously as he speaks and a sign language interpreter translates the lyrics of songs sung by the cantor.

Chapter 3

MOBILITY TRAINING

AN OVERVIEW

For disabled and nondisabled people alike, learning to travel in all conditions, on all types of vehicles, to ever-changing destinations, is a lifelong process. It includes seeking out key bits of relevant information, making use of appropriate assistance, and discovering through personal experience one's own travel interests, needs and capabilities. Individual travel patterns are influenced by each person's lifestyle, his social and emotional maturity, and occupational requirements.

Although some disabled people manage to teach themselves to travel entirely on their own, they are exceptions rather than the rule. Usually they are the people with mild rather than severe disabilities. Most disabled people require some assistance, guidance, or training as they struggle toward greater mobility, toward a reasonable level of self-reliance. For some, success is merely a matter of securing just enough training during the early stages of learning—or relearning—to travel. This builds a foundation for their own program of self-taught mobility, relying heavily on trial and error, learning through experimentation by their own mistakes. Then they advance nicely, tackling the world on their own. Others, however, cannot make significant headway without steady coaching over a period of months or even years.

Mobility training takes many forms, some easier to recognize than others. It may be obscured in various tasks, such as prescribing a wheelchair, or subtlely supplying emotional support when a student reaches an impasse, or helping a student to fill out an application for a special user's card for public transportation. It may be practical and concrete or intangible. It may take place directly or indirectly, in a formal or informal manner. It may be conducted systematically or haphazardly. It may or may not be tolerant of certain degrees of dependency. Ideally, mobility training blends in with other special education and rehabilitation services, coordination of effort being one of the keystones of a successful program.

Training may be carried out by a qualified instructor working alone, or by an instructor working with other professionals, or by caring people in the student's life, or some combination of these. It may be concentrated in daily lessons over a period of weeks, or in weekly or biweekly lessons spread over a year or more. The timetable varies with factors such as age, motivation, the type of environment, severity of disability, and the availability of people who teach mobility.

Mobility training includes all relevant details that enable a person to move safely and effectively from place to place. Its scope begins with teaching basic movement within a room and extends, through a series of small steps, to the complexities of long-distance travel. For every rung on the mobility ladder there is a corresponding one on the ladder of mobility training.

FOUR MAJOR CATEGORIES

Since mobility training entails the acquisition of a diversity of skills, it is useful to organize these skills into four major categories: (1) Indoor mobility skills; (2) Outdoor mobility skills; (3) Social skills; and (4) Complementary skills. These categories together comprise the essential building blocks of mobility training. The categories are not necessarily taught in a sequential order. Social and complementary skills, for example, might be interwoven with lessons devoted to indoor or outdoor mobility skills. Indoor skills, however, are most often taught first, before embarking on outdoor routes.

This four-unit model draws attention to the fact that effective travel is rooted in a combination of social, mental, and physical skills. Overemphasis on one set of skills to the exclusion of other sets—for whatever reason—is bound to miss the mark. Unless all four sets of skills are incorporated into a comprehensive program, the student's potential for travel will be only partially realized.

Indoor Mobility Skills

Indoor mobility refers to a person's movement from one spot to another within the bounds of any building. It includes such basic movement as getting around one's room and residence, learning to go up and down stairs, becoming aware of potential indoor hazards and how to avoid them. Getting around indoors may appear elementary, but for those in the throes of adjusting to a disability, indoor mobility may loom as a formidable obstacle requiring their utmost determination and perserverance. Picture a stroke patient painstakingly relearning to walk with a cane or walker, on inclines and declines as well as on flat surfaces. Since the danger of falling is always present, persistent effort and vigilance are essential. Quick results cannot be expected.

Indoor mobility represents the first in a long series of challenges along the path to independence. If the student cannot surmount indoor obstacles, he is less likely to manage higher hurdles further down the road. For this reason, indoor challenges, although deceptively simple, are a pivotal step in building confidence and in learning the entire range of travel skills. Indoor experiences offer the first chance for the student to derive a sense of accomplishment at mastering an arduous mobility task.

For a newly-disabled person, the challenges of indoor mobility represent the first and, not infrequently, the most difficult hurdle. Initial attempts at getting around a hospital or rehabilitation center may prove to be disheartening, and prompt the sad conclusion that independent travel is permanently out of reach. If such despair takes hold, the student may resist further efforts to navigate independently.

Evaluation of the student's travel strengths and weaknesses—an essential first step in training—usually begins indoors. What is the severity of his disability? At what age did it first occur? Is the student's disabling condition progressive or stable? In what specific ways does it interfere with his getting about? What are the student's present mobility habits? How does the student's family feel about independent travel? Did the student receive mobility instruction previously?

These and related questions beg for answers during an initial assessment, as the instructor constructs a preliminary profile of the student's mobility needs and assets. In a sense, the instructor takes a snapshot of the student's present level of functioning and uses that as a tentative starting point for individualized instruction. He obtains some of this information by reading the student's records, some by interviewing the family, while other answers must be elicited by talking to the student.

It is important for the instructor and parent to read and interpret the results of a current hearing test, particularly if the student is visually impaired, because the student must rely on his sense of hearing to localize sounds and make safe street crossings. If no hearing report is available, arrangements should be made for the student's hearing to be tested. And if the results are incomprehensible, a hearing specialist should be consulted for a professional interpretation. The mobility specialist can determine how specific auditory losses affect mobility by observing the student's reactions in various travel situations.

Similarly, it is valuable to study a current eye report to determine the specific boundaries of the student's visual fields. Someone with vision restricted at the bottom of his visual field might trip over curbs and benches, a fact that the instructor should be aware of before a mishap occurs. The eye report is best used in conjunction with the instructor's own evaluation of functional vision, as the instructor observes what the student can and cannot see under various lighting conditions in actual travel situations.

The instructor scrutinizes the student as he moves from place to place, usually on routes within a building, where travel is simpler and more sheltered than outdoors. What tasks are easily mastered, what tasks trigger a prolonged struggle? To a discerning eye, these observations reveal clues about the student's idiosyncracies and enable the instructor to pinpoint the student's needs and shape an effective teaching strategy centered on achievable objectives. Evaluation continues throughout the course of training, generating valuable feedback to the instructor for fine-tuning the direction of future lessons.

The pace of instruction, the speed at which lessons proceed, should be guided by a sensitive assessment of the student's emotional and physical readiness to cope with the stress of learning to travel. If the student's progress stalls, the best decision might be to back off and give the student time to collect himself before moving ahead, rather than pressing him harder to attend to the task at hand.

When training proceeds too slowly, it dampens the student's enthusiasm. Also, the instructor may become frustrated by his inability to achieve the results he had in mind. His frustration might manifest itself by unhelpful changes in his voice or manner. While such reactions are understandable, they are counterproductive. An alert instructor would recognize this all-too-human reaction and make appropriate adjustments.

The natural starting point for the mobility education of a disabled child is within his home. During the early, formative years, a mother cautions her toddler about what he can and cannot get into, teaches him how to cope with stairways, and how to avoid household hazards. As parents discern what their child can be reasonably expected to accomplish on his own, they set rules regarding the child's independent movement in and around the house. Parents sometimes receive assistance in this regard from a health care worker or teacher. Mobility education continues at school, with the help of a mobility specialist. Later in life, if needed, the student might benefit from being oriented to public buildings and his workplace by a specialist or by a helpful colleague.

For the person who becomes disabled as a teenager or adult, the early phases of mobility restoration focus on building bodily strength and coordination, moving about a hospital or rehabilitation center, going to therapy rooms, the dining area, and the lavatory. In time, the student tackles the task of getting around his home and later advances to public buildings.

Travel up and down stairs poses one of the toughest indoor challenges and requires careful practice to ensure safety. The student who cannot manage stairs on his own — for whatever reason — must find an alternative, such as an elevator. Escalators are a viable option for some people, but those who are wheelchair — mobile rarely use them.

As a blind student approaches a descending stairway, he probes with the tip of his cane to detect the edge of the top step and then anchors it there. He carefully slides his feet forward to the edge of the step and extends his toes slightly over the edge. In this way there is less chance of stumbling when he steps down. Holding onto a bannister and staying to the right are sound safety practices that could spell the difference between ease of movement and a mishap.

A recently-blinded person may experience paralyzing fear merely at the thought of approaching a stairway. If so, the instructor could alter the usual training sequence by postponing the objective of independence on stairs. That objective could be reserved for later phases of training when a basis for self-confidence had been established.

Whatever method of coping with stairs is chosen, it becomes an important part of an emergency plan for evacuating a building during fire drills or actual fires. For those traveling by bus or train, the proper procedure for emergency evacuation should be identified and practiced before a real emergency arises. Leaving the question of emergency evacuation unanswered may invite an avoidable tragedy.

Introducing a white cane to a newly-blinded person is a sensitive matter because the cane may be perceived as an upsetting stigma or an undesirable declaration of blindness. If the student still harbors hope of recovering his vision, or cringes at the thought of being identified as a blind person, he is likely to reject the cane and may turn his back on mobility training as well. If the blind person adamantly refuses to use a cane, he should consider other options, such as a guide dog or an electronic travel aid—or the possibility of arranging for the services of a human guide or a driver.

Among those born blind, the most difficult time to initiate cane travel is during adolescence, when any personal differences from other people are magnified and disturbing. Therefore, it is advisable to initiate cane travel before adolescence begins. Common sense indicates that a white cane should be forced on no one. Rather, it should be gradually drawn into a student's daily routine as he or she becomes ready to accept it and appreciate its functional value. A parent or instructor who insists that the student carry a cane at all times may unwittingly fuel a backlash against the cane.

Long canes are usually made of aluminum or fiberglass for strength, because they often bang against all kinds of obstacles, and lightness, because cane technique entails a continuous swinging motion. At the end of the aluminum cane is a nylon tip that resists wear as it scrapes along the pavement. The fiberglass cane has a ferrule tip, a rounded piece of metal that glides smoothly, even over rough surfaces. The aluminum cane is usually covered with a white reflective tape called scotchlite, and sometimes with a smaller strip of red at the bottom. Auto headlights reflect off the cane in the dark, making the traveler more visible to the driver.

The distance from the traveler's breastbone to the ground determines the correct length of the cane. This measurement gives rise to the term "prescription" or "long cane" because it is adjusted according to the height of each individual. This length allows the traveler to probe ahead about an extra pace while walking at an average clip. The traveler detects obstacles by swinging the cane in an arc as wide as his shoulders, and changes in ground level by touching the ground lightly at the end of each swing. It serves as an antenna or extension of the finger that stretches the traveler's sense of feeling to the tip of his cane. The length of the cane may create problems in congested areas if it pokes the feet of passersby and trips them. To avert this possibility, the traveler shortens the cane's length when in crowds by sliding his hand down the shaft of the cane.

During the summer of 1965 I had the privilege of serving as the first American mobility instructor to consult with officials in England about the value of using the long cane and associated cane techniques, as opposed to the shorter version preferred by them. Until that time, the blind people in England used a collapsible cane commonly called "the white stick," which was swung off to the side in no particular rhythm.

I was selected for this research project by the two sponsoring agencies, the American Foundation for the Blind in New York and the Royal National Institute for the Blind in London.

After teaching blind youngsters to travel with long canes at a residential school for the blind in Reigate, Surrey, I then worked with adult students at a rehabilitation center in Torquay, Devon. The results of this introductory course were favorable. The British went on to adopt the long cane and its techniques as a standard part of their mobility program because it provided superior protection.

Many partially sighted travelers who need the cane only occasionally prefer to use a folding cane. Held together by an elastic cord or a chain, its various sections can be pulled apart and collapsed into one length of about 12 inches. A folding or collapsible cane can be easily stored in a purse or pocket when not in use.

Most partially sighted students resist learning cane techniques. Uncertain about their usefulness, partially sighted students usually have little tolerance for practice sessions that call for repetitive swinging of the cane. They also tend to be more self-conscious about carrying a white cane than totally blind people are. Many partially sighted travelers simply hold a collapsible cane near their side, occasionally using it as a probe to confirm the location of an obstacle or a change in ground level. Rather than as a travel tool, some people carry a white cane primarily to identify themselves as being visually impaired, in hopes that other people will more readily extend helpful courtesies.

Choosing among types of canes is a personal matter and no one should force the student to use a cane that makes him feel uncomfortable. The student should try out each type of cane and then select the one best suited for his purpose.

To illustrate some aspects of indoor training, here is a glimpse into the life of Mary, a 10-year-old blind girl. Recently, she moved into a new neighborhood and faces the task of learning to find her way around her new elementary school. A mobility instructor employed by the Board of Education arranged to meet her on her first morning at school to orient her to the entire building by teaching her routes from her classroom to the lavatory, the office, the library—so she could form a mental picture of the school.

The instructor reserved special attention for potential danger spots, such as stairways and doors that might suddenly swing open. He taught her a way of using her arm and hand to protect the upper part of her body when she senses an object protruding from a wall, such as a fire extinguisher. She holds her arm across her body at shoulder level, holding the arm about a foot in front of her, so that her arm would contact an object before the object strikes her face. This timely and patient orientation, extending over several days, strengthened her sense of security. This in turn reduced anxiety for Mary and for those responsible for her well-being.

At this stage in her development, Mary must rely on a specialist, a teacher, or parent to become familiar with new surroundings. But as she gains experience, she will be able to familiarize herself with new buildings, seeking from others only specific bits of information she cannot ascertain for herself.

The instructor discovered that her cane was too short for her needs. She had outgrown it, so he gave her a longer one. He also arranged to talk with her mother about his plans for mobility training and to solicit her views on the subject.

A student who is retarded also benefits from a helping hand in becoming familiar with the interior of a building or worksite. If the building in question is large, it should be divided into subsections for instructional purposes, the student mastering one section before advancing to the next. Task simplification—breaking complex assignments into manageable pieces—is always a helpful principle.

Effective instruction is characterized by a flow of concrete words and directions, rather than speaking in general or abstract terms. Repetition of each teaching step is an educational virtue which paves the way for trouble-free trips. The importance of reassuring repetition in mobility training cannot be overemphasized. In addition, the prudent use of verbal praise boosts the student's spirits, as does appropriate physical contact, such as a pat on the back.

Likewise with a person in a wheelchair, timely guidance on indoor routes comes in handy, along with advise on ways to circumvent thorny problems such as coping with stairs. With experience, the wheelchair user masters the knack of familiarizing himself with buildings he enters for the first time.

Physical therapists and occupational therapists prescribe the size and type of wheelchair best suited for the student's needs. In consultation with physicians, they recommend the best combination of walking aids: braces, crutches, cane, or walkers. Walkers are used for support while walking indoors and outdoors. The person leans forward on the four-legged device and lifts it slightly off the ground to get set for the next step. Made of lightweight aluminum, some walkers feature wheels on the bottom of the two front legs for easier gliding, and some walkers are collapsible so disabled people can carry them more easily when going up or down stairs.

Physical therapists work with people having all sorts of physical problems: strokes, broken hips, muscular weaknesses, and arthritis. Physical therapy is a relatively young field that grew largely out of World War I, when large numbers of injured soldiers required rehabilitation. Therapists in those days were known as reconstruction aides.

Physical therapists supervise progressive exercises for increasing upper and lower body strength, for correcting faulty posture, and for increasing the degree of joint mobility. They set a high priority on making the patient ambulatory. They might cheer on a patient will full leg braces who struggles to regain use of his legs while walking between parallel bars. Some exercises begin while the patient is still confined to bed after illness or injury. They teach patients to transfer their bodies from a bed to a wheelchair and from a wheelchair to a car. This manuever requires coordination, strength, and painstaking practice to accomplish safely. Although they offer pointers about outdoor travel, their work focuses on indoor mobility within a hospital or rehabilitation center. The patient must experiment for himself regarding many aspects of outdoor travel.

Occupational therapists teach self-help skills such as learning to dress, groom, and feed oneself. While much of occupational therapy takes the form of craft work and recreational activities, occupational therapists also strive to mobilize stiff joints and to increase muscle power through the use of graduated exercises. They participate in mobility training by helping the patient to complete the transition from a medical facility to a reasonably normal life in his community. But, like physical therapists, their primary concern is limited to indoor mobility.

Physical therapists and occupational therapists supervise the safe use of elevators, timing the student to ensure that he can enter or exit the elevator before the doors close. They monitor his readiness to travel on a given floor in a hospital or rehabilitation center, through the entire building, and then on selected outdoor routes. They correct balance, posture, and gait problems, and work toward increasing stamina. Rhythmic activities accompanied by music are sometimes used to encourage movement. Patients sometimes play simple musical instruments, adding an element of fun to the arduous task of learning to move and develop muscle coordination. Some rehabilitation programs employ a music therapist for this purpose.

An occupational therapist might visit the student's home to check for unnecessary architectural barriers. Are scatter rugs lying around waiting for an accident to happen? Should a handrail be installed along some walls so a person with unsteady gait could hold on to it for support? Do the walls need to be reinforced first? Flat-weave carpeting makes it easier to manuever a chair. Curbless showers and low sinks are practical modifications, along with wider doorways and hallways. It might be desirable to install a system that melts snow and ice under driveways and outdoor ramps. After surveying the patient's home and surroundings, perhaps in conjunction with an architect or rehabilitation engineer, the occupational therapist recommends appropriate modifications.

People with paralyzed lower limbs (paraplegia) and those who have lost significant use of all four limbs (quadriplegia) sometimes use electric wheelchairs powered by batteries. These motorized chairs, carts, and three-wheeled scooters, some of which are compact and portable, can be operated by slight pressure on a sensitive control lever, also known as a "joy stick." Some wheelchairs have specially equipped control systems that a person with quadriplegia can operate by mouth and teeth movements, or by blowing and sucking on a tube. Getting about indoors affords good opportunities for mastering the intricacies of specialized controls in a sheltered setting.

Advances in computer technology in the 1980s have spawned numerous aids and appliances that ease the difficulties of daily life for many severely disabled people. A wireless microphone, voice-activated and hooked up to a computer, controls the opening and closing of doors, turns appliances on and off, and regulates room temperature and humidity. Special telephones signal an operator when the user simply blows into a tube. Up-to-the-minute technology enables those with limited dexterity to retrieve food from a top shelf and transfer from wheelchair to toilet or bathtub or bed with electronically-controlled lifts.

Other useful modifications include: kitchen counters lower than normal and vacant beneath, so the wheelchair user can scoot underneath; kitchen cabinets that can be lowered from their standard height to counter level; shelves that slide out from a below-the-counter refrigerator, allowing the tenant to fetch food that was pushed to the back; and closet racks that can be pulled down to bring a shirt or pair of slacks within reach.

If a student with a physical impairment cannot move easily through crowded corridors, it might be wise to make special arrangements. Susan, for example, a 14-year-old student in an urban high school, injured her leg in a skiing accident. She walked with crutches, but still struggled to keep her balance. Unsteady and unsure of herself, she was afraid of being jostled while threading her way through clusters of energetic students. Sometimes she felt like skipping school rather than facing the hectic hallways.

Recognizing this problem, her homeroom teacher permitted Susan to change classes five minutes before the usual time, when hallways were empty. The teacher was sensitive enough to include Susan's friend, Billy, in this arrangement, just in case she needed help and for social support, so Susan would not feel isolated. As her confidence grew, Susan was eased into the regular class-change schedule.

A vital concern for a deaf person is to recognize emergency signals such as fire alarms. Most alarms, however, are based on auditory signals. A loud clanging of bells or a shrill buzzer alert hearing people to imminent danger, but have no practical value for deaf people. To remedy this oversight, auditory signals must be converted into visual cues, such as bright, flashing lights. In buildings frequented by deaf people, visual adaptations of alarms are an essential safety measure and warrant serious attention from building management.

The ideas presented here about indoor mobility also apply to multiply disabled people, those with unique combinations of physical and mental impairments. The value of these ideas depend on how carefully they are tailored to meet each student's individual needs. Mobility training with multiply disabled students poses special challenges to the instructor's resourcefulness. It also presents abundant opportunities to render assistance where it is clearly needed. To meet those challenges, the instructor draws on his knowledge of each separate disability, continually assessing its effect on the student's overall functioning. At the same time, he bears in mind the effect generated by the combined disabilities.

Outdoor Mobility Skills

Outdoor mobility training comprises the entire range of skills necessary for travel to any destination beyond one's front door. Beginning with a quick trip to the corner grocery store, it extends to travel through all kinds of neighborhoods—from sparsely populated residential neighborhoods to crowded business and shopping districts. From quiet country roads to congested city intersections, street crossings constitute a crucial part of outdoor training, as does the use of all forms of public transportation.

The early phases of outdoor training for a disabled child closely parallel those of a nondisabled child. Usually parents acquaint their child with the area around his residence: first the yard or play area adjacent to an apartment building, the way to the nearest corner and then around the block. According to his physical and emotional readiness, the child is permitted to cross only those streets he or she can manage with a high degree of certainty, once safety precautions have been thoroughly explained. Ideally, a mobility specialist would teach neighborhood travel skills, but often these initial steps are supervised by parents or other family members, such as a brother or sister.

An instructor or parent cautions the child to cross streets only at the corner—not from the middle of the block or from between parked cars, which would increase the chance of being hit by a vehicle. The exception to this safety practice is a wheelchair user who must roll down a driveway because there is no curb cut at the corner. In that case, the traveler would be advised to remain especially alert for oncoming cars.

Parents specify what time of day their child is permitted to cross a particular street and when he is forbidden to do so. A partially-sighted boy, for example, who easily crosses a street near his home during the day is barred from doing so after dark, when he no longer can rely on his remaining vision. Certain streets with heavy traffic might be placed off-limits during rush hours. There is no substitute for good judgement and old-fashioned common sense when making these decisions.

Functional vision vacillates with lighting conditions. Some people see best on bright, sunny days while others see more clearly on cloudy days. A person with retinitis pigmentosa (a disorder of the retina), sees better on cloudy days than on bright days. Someone with tunnel vision (central vision but no side vision) learns to direct his vision in the most effective way. Color blind people should learn that the red light on a tricolored traffic signal is usually the top light. This knowledge makes them less dependent on color identification. It is important for the traveler and his family to become aware of these and similar idiosyncrasies and to recognize their implications for travel.

Here are some points to keep in mind when a child begins traveling alone: The child should know his full address and phone number, including area code. A nonverbal child should carry a card or wear an inscribed bracelet with this basic information. He must understand that it should be shown only to a trusted adult, someone wearing a uniform, such as a policeman, mailman, or bus driver, and only then for good reason. The child may not comprehend that someone would intentionally harm him, so this requires some explanation. Bags containing valuables should not be hung on a wheelchair handle where they would be easy targets for thieves. To test the child's understanding of these precautions, observe him as he travels, rather than relying solely on his verbal description of the correct response.

The youngster should also know what to do if he gets lost, how to cope with ridicule, how to deal with a mugging or sexual molestation, and how to stave off an abduction attempt. It is helpful for parents to discuss these concerns with other parents, a counselor, or a mobility specialist.

An informed family participates as working members of the mobility training team. The instructor discusses each objective with the student's parents and invites them to observe lessons and monitor progress. Parents may help select routes and supervise the student's practice runs between lessons, sharing with the instructor their observations about persistent snags. Parental involvement sharpens their judgment about when to widen travel boundaries.

As the instructor gets better acquainted with the parents' perspective on their child's independence, he can pinpoint problems and revise his teaching strategy. Communication and cooperation between instructor and parents yield valuable benefits for the young student, just as they do for adult students when family members take an active interest.

Delaying the time when a youngster travels alone is understandable, but extended delay hampers his growth of self-confidence and travel skills. Overprotection is counterproductive in the long run, even when rooted in good intentions. Prolonged reluctance to grant freedom may stem from overanxiety, from imagining that the youngster flirts with danger whenever no parent or family member watches over him. Parents may not be fully aware of their youngster's travel capabilities and potential. Those who have not fully accepted their child's disability may feel embarrassed by attention directed at them or at their child as his mobility increases.

Some parents worry about what neighbors think about a disabled child traveling alone. They try to second-guess whether neighbors would perceive them as being negligent or foolhardy by allowing their child to travel without supervision. In doing so, they unintentionally hinder their child's development.

Clinging to the illusion that their child's disability will miraculously disappear, or somehow be "cured," whittles away the motivation to work toward self-reliance—for both the child and his family. False hopes dilute the sustained determination essential for acquiring mobility skills. Parents' illusions distort the child's thinking about his future. I once worked with a partially sighted 10-year-old boy who frowned on taking mobility lessons. When I walked into his classroom, he grimaced to display his disdain for mobility training. His teacher and I explained that basic skills learned now would enable him to travel independently later in life. He answered defiantly that when he got old enough, he would drive his own car. He cited his stepfather as the authority who had assured him that his vision would become normal during adolescence. Eventually, he warmed up to the lessons and learned to travel several routes in the school neighborhood, discovering that it was fun to cross streets alone and take an occasional trip to a candy store.

Parents may refuse to accept the inevitable risks attached to adolescence, to every bumpy road leading to adulthood. High anxiety may occur at every milestone on the way to independence. Parents may send out a message, perhaps unintentionally or unconsciously, that travel is dangerous, that preparing for self-reliance should be avoided, or at least delayed as long as possible.

Parents naturally take into account the character of their neighborhood when making decisions about solo trips. Greater precautions are required if they live in or near a large city, where the danger of being mugged or molested is ever-present. But precautions are even more urgent for a disabled person because he may be less able to defend himself or escape quickly. The overall timetable for granting independence is influenced by customary practices for unsupervised travel in each neighborhood.

Many disabled people travel well enough to lead a full and satisfying life. But their pace of maturation may be slow, with prolonged periods of dependent mobility. Highly mobile people in all walks of life, with every conceivable disability, testify by their actions that freedom of mobility is no idle dream for those determined to grapple with inevitable problems and to come out a winner! Inspiring stories about the accomplishments of disabled people appear regularly in the media. Just one example: A young man in a wheelchair, eager to prove his vitality to himself and to the world, spent 26 months traveling around the world in his wheelchair!

Children who spend their early years in an institution ordinarily fall below standards of independence that shape the mobility habits of their peers who live at home. In residential schools for the blind and some institutions for the retarded, however, greater attention has been focused during the past two decades on fostering independence. Self-help programs that include mobility training have been established, attesting to the growing importance of independent travel in the eyes of administrators.

Learning a Route

Outdoor mobility training is usually organized in units called routes. A route is a purposefully chosen course from a starting to finishing point, a strategy for getting from point A to point B. The instructor selects routes suited to the student's skills and relevant to his interests and needs. He choses a series of routes that progresses from simple, straightforward routes to more complicated ones.

The instructor walks through several possible routes and appraises potential hazards before deciding on the most suitable route. When working with a youngster, the instructor might select a route that includes a street crossing where a crossing guard or police officer is posted, or one with built-in motivation, like a friend's house or a candy store.

He familiarizes himself with all aspects of the chosen route before attempting to teach it. Ideally, the instructor would travel through the route while simulating the student's disabling condition: with a blindfold, if the student is blind; in a wheelchair, if the student uses one. In this way, the instructor would perceive problems from the traveler's viewpoint and be better prepared to discuss them.

The instructor begins work with the student by describing the route: the starting point, distances between changes of direction, landmarks (for blind students, ones that could be identified by hearing, smell, or touch), potential hazards, and the termination point. There is more to learning a route than simply memorizing a series of street names. In winter, directions would include suggestions about shelter from wind, rain, snow, and in the summer, from intense sunshine.

An initial description includes details about the physical characteristics of the surrounding neighborhood. Are there mostly office buildings or houses or a mixture of the two? Do streets intersect at right angles or diagonally? Photographs and simple maps of the area provide an overview of the neighborhood and reduce the chance of getting confused or lost.

Directions should be clear, concise, and concrete, the clutter of unnecessary details weeded out. Some students retain directions better by writing them down. If the student repeats the directions before taking his first step, mental errors can easily be spotted and corrected. This serves as a double-check on his understanding and retention of the directions.

A student who is uncertain about the route should be asked to describe it at the beginning of each lesson, especially if he has struggled with the same route for several lessons. If he has difficulty with a particular section, it should be discussed thoroughly, the instructor suggesting various approaches to the problem.

Discussions also take place after the route is completed as instructor and student figure out why something went wrong. An after-the-lesson chat provides a more relaxed atmosphere than if the instructor stops to explain every problem in the middle of a route. Mental preparation before each lesson and casual review after each lesson facilitate progress.

While going through the route for the first time, the instructor shadows the student, staying close by, assisting only when necessary. As the student's competence grows, the instructor gradually increases his distance from the student. Lengthy or difficult routes may be divided into subsections, each section becoming a miniroute that must be mastered before advancing to the next section. The decision about subdividing a route is based on the instructor's judgement regarding how much information the student can absorb at one time.

The route is repeated until the student can travel alone with assurance and safety. For students who are mentally retarded, repetition continues to the point of overlearning, to ensure that they can manage it safely and consistently. In the process of learning routes, the relationship between student and instructor grows. They get to know and trust one another as shared experiences accumulate.

As the instructor pulls further away, he has a better chance to observe the student's interaction with the public, as people approach him offering help, or when the student initiates contact. This separation also provides room for the unexpected to happen. As it does, the student's reactions can be observed and later discussed.

If the route involves travel on a bus, the instructor, in the later phases of training, might follow in a car. This gives a student the feeling of traveling alone, while the instructor still has the opportunity to observe him. By exposing the student to a wide variety of situations during training, it is less likely the student will feel stress-bound when new situations arise after training ends.

The public, unaware of his training role, sometimes misinterprets the instructor's laid-back manner as a callous refusal to assist a disabled person. Some people frown at him or even question why he doesn't do something instead of just standing there, staring at the disabled person. The instructor either ignores these reactions or explains his perplexing behavior, according to the situation and his teaching style. Years ago, some agencies for the blind required mobility instructors to wear identifying arm bands, but that practice has virtually disappeared. Now, each instructor corrects misconceptions in his own way.

I once worked with a teenaged blind girl in a business district, following a few paces behind her as I closely observed her cane technique. Suddenly, two plainclothes detectives stopped me to ask why I was following her. After producing some identification and asking my student to verify that I was her instructor, they allowed me to proceed with the lesson. Apparently, someone had become suspicious after observing me follow the girl and called the police. It was all in a day's work.

The final step is taken when the student goes through the route independently, without being observed at all. Until a successful solo trip is completed, the next route is not attempted. The instructor must use critical judgment in deciding when the student is ready to travel the route alone.

Once a route is completed, the instructor may reverse the procedure by directing the student to travel the same route beginning from the end and finishing at the starting point. This is a useful way to build on the student's knowledge of the route while challenging him to envision it from a different perspective. Reversing the route also presents a new set of problems, even though the student already knows it from one direction.

The most exciting part of training occurs when the student begins solo voyages. As solo-time approaches, the emotions of both student and instructor intensify: Mild apprehension mingles with anticipatory joy at the prospect of achieving a coveted goal. The instructor knows the student has butterflies in his stomach, but he helps him keep the butterflies in formation, as attention becomes riveted on the task.

After the first solo trip, exhilaration is the mood of the day. Both student and instructor feel as if they had scaled a mountain. It seems for the moment as though they were the only ones ever to do so. This accomplishment gratifies the instructor and motivates the student to tackle remaining routes, his self-confidence now bolstered. Not infrequently, a new-found pride shines through the student's general appearance as he or she spruces up and smiles more. As these adventures continue, the bond between student and instructor strengthens, building a stockpile of trust, respect, and appreciation for one another.

The student learns alternative routes to the same destination, choosing on the basis of his experience the one that presents the fewest problems. He might prefer one route at a certain time and another during rush hour. A wheelchair user selects a route with the fewest curbs and stairs. A visually impaired traveler chooses a route with the fewest turns and least congested sidewalks. A retarded traveler sticks to the least complicated route.

As training on various routes continues, some transfer of learning can be expected: What the student learned on one route may help him as he attempts subsequent routes. With practice, the student becomes more adept at memorizing a series of street names.

The student increasingly takes more responsibility for his travel. He makes subtle variations on the same route. He learns to adapt to weather conditions, including high winds, bright sun, rain, and snow. He works out a strategy for coping with ice-covered sidewalks. As experience accumulates, he discovers untapped resources within himself for coping with the ever-changing challenges of independent travel.

Street Crossings

No two ways about it, street crossings are tricky and potentially dangerous. Even the most alert nondisabled traveler encounters unexpected, menacing problems: A car runs a stop sign or red light; a drunken driver smashes into a turning truck, sending debris whizzing through passing pedestrians; an accelerator jams, causing an automobile to careen into a cluster of pedestrians. Drivers who flagrantly disobey traffic laws create hazards that loom even larger for disabled travelers. Impaired vision or hearing obscures warning signals, shaving vital seconds off reaction times. Diminished bodily strength hinders quick evasive actions. For the disabled traveler, street crossings require planning, practice, and unflagging alertness.

The variety of streets is endless. Some are narrow with sporadic bursts of traffic. Some are wide boulevards with six or eight lanes of steadily-moving cars, trucks, and buses. Still others fall between these extremes. A median divides some wide streets, providing a safety zone in the middle of the crossing.

The traveler must base his judgement about making a safe crossing on a realistic assessment. As he scans the traffic pattern and the width of the street, the traveler must calculate his physical limitations and the potential dangers. If a wheelchair user underestimates the time needed to cross a wide street, he might be threatened by accelerating cars before reaching the opposite curb. It is prudent for the traveler in a wheelchair to make eye contact with the driver of a car about to turn in front of him, so they have a tacit understanding about what moves each is about to make. The person in a wheelchair may decide to wave on a driver in order to clear his path to the curb. If the traveler doubts his chances for a safe crossing for any reason, he would be well-advised to seek assistance from passersby, who are usually more than willing to help.

While waiting to cross, the person in a wheelchair positions himself at the top of the curb cut, not at the bottom near the edge of the street. This position serves two purposes: first, he removes himself from the danger of being run over by the wheels of turning vehicles, and second, he gains momentum by rolling down the slope.

Some blind pedestrians habitually veer into parallel traffic as they cross the street. This tendency is as common as it is dangerous. Maintaining a straight direction is difficult for a blind traveler, especially if he walks slowly. The problem of veering while crossing warrants special attention and practice during mobility lessons to prevent its recurrence.

Traffic laws in some states permit vehicles to turn right at specified intersections when facing a red light. While this law, known as "right-on-red," facilitates the flow of traffic, it compounds traffic hazards for disabled pedestrians. They cannot count on predictable traffic patterns. To add to the confusion, some traffic lights permit right or left turns when a green arrow appears. Clear explanations and practice are required to safeguard the traveler at intersections with these features.

Before stepping into a street, it is important to look to the right and left, and continue looking both ways until reaching the opposite curb. This is the best way to protect against vehicles that turn unexpectedly into the pedestrian's path. Since this precaution does not develop naturally for most disabled travelers, especially youngsters, the instructor should emphasize it during lessons until looking both ways becomes a habit. Being unaware of potential dangers while crossing spells trouble for the unsuspecting pedestrian.

Another feature that deserves attention is the button on some traffic lights that, when pushed, reduces the time spent waiting for a green light. The student learns where the button is located and when to use it. He also learns that the two parallel white lines extending from corner to corner outline the safest crossing lane. From a legal standpoint, a traveler involved in an accident has a stronger case if he is struck while crossing within the white lines.

By stepping into a street while waiting for traffic to clear, the traveler exposes himself to passing traffic, especially where right-on-red is in effect. The safest practice is to remain on the curb until the path is entirely clear. The chance of stumbling when stepping off a curb is reduced if the blind traveler locates the curb with the tip of his cane and brings both feet near the edge, in the same manner used for locating the edge of descending stairs. If his toes rest right on the edge at a busy intersection, however, he risks having them run over by a turning bus or truck.

Bicycles pose a surprising threat to any pedestrian's safety and composure, but even more so to the disabled traveler's. The threat is worsened when cyclists whiz around corners, behaving as if they are above traffic laws. It is difficult to enforce the patchwork of local regulations and ordinances governing bicycle riders. The instructor should alert his students to these two-wheeled dangers.

A few traffic lights in America are equipped with bells or buzzers that sound when all traffic is stopped, indicating to sightless pedestrians a safe time to cross. One such arrangement exists at a large intersection in Watertown, Massachusetts, near the Perkins School for the Blind. Also, the city council of a small town in California recently voted to install bells on all traffic lights within the town's limits.

In Sweden, Australia, and New Zealand, auditory signals are more commonplace than in America. In Auckland, New Zealand, auditory signals were installed about 10 years ago at major intersections as an aid for all pedestrians, not only for the disabled. City officials believe the buzzer alerts the average pedestrian to step off quickly at the right moment. By prompting the crossings of all pedestrians during the first few seconds of the buzzer, the chance for accidents is reduced.

Opinions regarding the value of audible traffic signals are divided. Some people contend that the ringing masks traffic sounds, or fear that blind people might depend on the signals and then become confused in their absence. Others argue that special adaptations draw unfavorable attention to blind people, disparaging their capability for executing such basic tasks as crossing a street. Proponents of this point of view call for removal of audible traffic signals and other environmental modifications that perpetuate the notion that blind people are incapable of leading a normal life. Audible traffic signals remain a controversial aid for travelers who are visually impaired.

The instructor should acquaint his students with the physical details and traffic patterns at each intersection along a route. If it is a one-way street, which way does the traffic flow? How wide is the street? Does one street dead end into another? Is the curb rounded or square? Where are the curb cuts? Is there a traffic light, a stop sign, or a traffic cop? Are left turns prohibited by the law at certain times?

Relying on his sense of hearing, the visually impaired student must detect a clear break in the traffic flow before crossing. This is more easily accomplished at intersections with traffic lights because they regulate traffic flow in a more predictable pattern. As the student faces a red light, he listens carefully to the sound of idling motors in the street parallel to his path.

When the traffic surges forward, it indicates that the light facing him just turned green and he can cross, provided no cars are turning. The safest time to start crossing is during the first few seconds after cars accelerate, because that ensures the longest interval with the green light. This practice also prevents the dangerous mistake of stepping off just as the green cycle ends. Repetitive practice is needed to ensure that the student doesn't misinterpret traffic sounds and step into the street at the wrong moment. The blind traveler continues listening to traffic cues as he crosses, to avoid veering into parallel traffic or bumping into a turning car. If the traveler is partially sighted, he continues listening to traffic and looking both ways until reaching the opposite curb.

The instructor positions himself directly in back of the student, close enough to stop the student if he inadvertently passes too close to a vehicle. If he stood on either side of the student, he might interfere with the student's hearing or vision, or simply distract him.

Some intersections with left-turn arrows and right-on-red are so confusing that the instructor should spend time standing with the student on a corner, observing the traffic pattern, listening to various lanes of traffic, explaining irregularities, reviewing safety rules and answering the student's questions. This practice is especially valuable for blind students who need time to get their bearings and build their confidence.

While training a congenitally blind teenager in Michigan, I tried in vain to explain how a traffic light controls traffic flow on two intersecting streets. One street had heavier traffic than the other. Despite all my explanations, she remained baffled, so I decided to time the light cycle. When I told her that the busier street had a green light for 30 seconds and the quieter one for 20 seconds, she looked disconcerted and said with indignation, "I think every street should have equal opportunity." Although this incident took place 25 years ago, it still makes me smile.

Since travelers who are visually impaired rely on their sense of hearing, they should keep their ears free from external obstructions. If a hood is worn, it should be removed when preparing to cross and while crossing. The same holds true for ear muffs and ear plugs from portable radios or cassette players, which should not be worn at any time while a blind person travels alone. The student also learns not to cross when he hears unusually loud noises, such as the chattering of a jackhammer, the drone of a low flying plane, or the testing of an emergency warning system. Loud sounds mask vital traffic cues, so the student must wait until unusual noises quiet down before crossing. Deaf students, on the other hand, unable to use auditory cues, must rely completely on visual alertness and mental concentration.

The sirens of police cars, fire engines, and ambulances deserve special mention. The student should learn that all vehicles are required by law to pull over to the right and stop when a siren sounds, and that no pedestrians should enter an intersection until the siren fades away. Knowledge of this safety precaution may prevent an accident.

At a corner without a traffic light, the traveler may hear an idling motor nearby and become impatient about waiting for the car to pass. Nevertheless, the traveler should resist the temptation to cross while the sound of the motor can still be heard. The driver may have spotted the traveler and decided to let him cross. But a blind person cannot afford to accept this courtesy, because the idling motor might mask the sound of another oncoming vehicle whose driver might not see the blind person starting to cross. In the early stages of training, the instructor would wave on the waiting car. In time, the student becomes adept at signaling with a hand motion, communicating directly with the driver by means of an informal sign language his intention to let him pass.

A well-meaning driver or passerby might shout, "Go ahead and cross; you're OK now." Such promptings should never serve as the sole basis for a decision to cross. The solicitous onlooker might be aware of only one lane of traffic and unaware that another car is about to pass, posing an imminent danger. Or a well-meaning but insensitive pedestrian might shove a blind person forward when the traffic signal turns green or even pull him along by his cane. The blind traveler must hold his ground and refuse to be pushed or pulled in any direction. These are examples of the mental discipline required of any prudent traveler.

The wise traveler resists the temptation to follow pedestrians who cross whenever there is the slightest opening, even against a red light or a flashing "Don't Walk" sign. He knows that other pedestrians are not a reliable cue. For safety's sake, the disabled traveler must learn to think for himself or herself, make on-the-spot decisions, and act independently. Aside from being injured in an accident, losing a lawsuit due to contributory negligence is just one undesirable result of ignoring safety rules and common sense.

Recently, a blind couple tried to cross an eight lane boulevard at dusk in Washington, D.C. where there was no traffic light. Just as they reached the last lane, a car struck them, killing the couple. Special precautions must be taken at dusk and in hours of darkness. More than half of all traffic fatalities occur during hours of darkness, even though traffic is more sparse, and fewer pedestrians venture out at night. The majority of pedestrians killed in traffic accidents contribute to their own fate by violating a traffic law or committing an obviously unsafe act.

For some blind people, the best way to cross streets is with a trusted guide dog in harness at their side. Guide dogs are rigorously trained for months by an instructor who often wears a blindfold himself while working with the dog. Each blind student spends about a month getting acquainted with his new companion in all kinds of travel situations under the watchful eye of his trainer. As if by instinct, the dog stops at curbs, threads a safe path through crowds, veers away from impending danger, such as low awnings or other overhangs, and is always careful about protecting its master. Schooled in intelligent disobedience, the dog ignores commands that would imperil its master. If the command "Forward!" is given as a car approaches, the dog remains on its haunches until traffic on the street clears. Despite these remarkable traits, the master remains in charge, determining which route to take. It is a mistake to believe that the dog decides where to take the master.

Exaggerated ideas about canine capabilities have produced a host of jokes, such as the one about a blind man who attends a movie with his guide dog, which responds with an astonishing display of emotions, crying and laughing in all the right places. As they walk out of the theater, an observer remarks, "It was just amazing the way your dog thoroughly enjoyed that show." The blind man replies, "Yes, I was surprised too. He didn't like the book at all!"

Guide dogs garner high marks from their masters (and from fascinated onlookers) for their effectiveness and companionship. A special law entitles blind people to enter restaurants with guide dogs, even though all other dogs are prohibited. The working life of a guide dog is about seven years, after which time many blind travelers return to their guide dog school for about a week to join with a new canine partner. Second, third and fourth dogs are not uncommon.

The percentage of blind people who use guide dogs remains small, about 2 percent of people with visual impairments. This surprisingly low figure stems from eligibility criteria for perspective users: the applicant must be beyond high school age, so as to be responsible enough to care for the dog, but not elderly, due to the stamina necessary to keep up with the animal. (The majority of visually impaired people are over the age of 60.) Only those with total blindness or very limited vision are accepted. People with better vision would not rely sufficiently on the dog to maintain its working form. (Less than 10 percent of all legally blind people are totally blind.) On a more personal level, the prospective user must be willing to spend considerable time every day walking and caring for the dog. Guide dog schools usually don't accept deaf-blind applicants, but exceptions are occasionally made.

Guide dogs for blind travelers are not the only animals trained to help disabled people. About 10,000 service dogs assist people who are hearing impaired, visually impaired, and physically disabled. Hearing dogs for deaf people, usually puppies and young adult dogs, must be friendly, playful, and have an acute sense of hearing. Through positive reinforcement, a hearing dog learns that his primary responsibility is to respond to his master's voice and hand signals. Some of the more unusual services performed by these four-footed workers include responding to a microwave oven timer, a smoke detector, and a doorbell, and reminding owners about dinner.

Labradors, golden retrievers, and German shepherds are trained to help people with physical disabilities by pushing and pulling a wheelchair, retrieving objects and even turning hard-to-reach light switches on and off. These service dogs can carry small bags from a clerk to a disabled customer, pick up the telephone, and open doors. Demand for these canine companions is so great that interested applicants must anticipate a lengthy waiting period.

Trained capuchin monkeys help people with quadraplegia to perform daily chores, even lending a hand with shopping. Weighing between 7 and 12 pounds, they are intelligent, have good memories, and life expectancies of about 30 years. Owners often discover that monkeys are a social asset, as strangers approach to chat about the unusual helpers.

A person who is both totally blind and totally deaf can learn to use a cane to find his way to a street corner, but a mobility instructor would advise him not to cross alone, since a sightless traveler must rely on his hearing to cross safely. There are, however, several ways a deaf-blind traveler can seek assistance. If he can speak, he requests help orally. If not, he can carry a set of cards with requests, written in large letters, such as, "I AM DEAF & BLIND. Please help me across Main Street. Tap me on the shoulder if you understand. Thank You!" The traveler may have a braille index on the cards, so he can quickly locate the card he wants. By carrying a separate set of cards for each route, a deaf-blind traveler is more assured of enlisting precisely the help he needs, without getting tangled in communication difficulties.

People who are deaf, retarded, or speech impaired could also benefit by using similar cards to reduce or eliminate frustration and embarrassment while communicating. This is an example of an adaptive technique, designed for one specific disability group, that can benefit dissimilar groups.

Street crossings are made easier for wheelchair riders by curb cuts, slopes that enable a person in a wheelchair to roll from sidewalk level to street level. They serve the purpose best if they are not angled too steeply and are not too narrow. Curb cuts have been cropping up at increasing numbers of street corners across America as appreciation of their value grows, and as advocacy groups press for their installation. Where curb cuts do not exist, the traveler must get help from someone or lower himself to the street level by jumping the curb, a risky feat that requires considerable strength.

A person in a wheelchair must gauge both the speed of oncoming traffic and his own top speed. He must judge which crossings are manageable and which pose an unacceptable risk. In reaching this judgement, he takes into account the condition of the road surface, since many streets are rutted and gouged, making it difficult to control the direction and balance of the wheelchair.

Elderly people who walk slowly are especially vulnerable while crossing streets and must be mindful of their limitations. Since they may need help crossing streets, they should learn when to ask for assistance, even if it means swallowing a lifetime of pride.

People with retardation are capable of crossing streets alone, but the extent of their independence varies with the severity of impairment. Moderately retarded travelers learn to cross streets after receiving pointers from family members, friends, or a mobility specialist. The student may need tips on what to do if he finds himself in the middle of the street when a car suddenly turns in front of him. There are no sweeping guidelines regarding whether severely retarded students can cross busy streets. Each student must be evaluated and given the benefit of training before permanent restrictions can be responsibly imposed.

If no mobility specialist is available for an assessment, the student might be evaluated by some other professional person, such as a teacher or an occupational therapist. Or a disabled peer might offer advise and encouragement with the hope that others can benefit from his experience. Parents, brothers, sisters, and friends can also assist with various aspects of evaluation and training.

A student with retardation needs a thorough understanding of traffic safety rules, such as don't cross from the middle of the block or from between parked cars, jaywalking is dangerous, and so on. The student must realize that mistakes or confusion during street crossings have dire consequences.

The student learns to anticipate the unexpected and comes to realize that drivers don't always obey traffic laws. It takes time to learn the subtleties of traffic patterns, such as the increase in traffic during certain times of the day, and the corresponding changes in traffic signals.

Before attempting to cross alone, the student should experience crossing streets while accompanied by a responsible adult. The shift to independence should be made gradually, the helper accompanying the student half way across until the student is confident enough to walk the entire width of the street unassisted.

It can never be assumed that the student knows all the relevant facts about streets and traffic, so each detail should be checked out. On a traffic light, what do the colors red, green, and yellow signify? Which traffic light controls which intersecting street? Why do drivers stop at stop signs? What is a one-way street? Teaching these concepts should be coupled with practice in real traffic situations.

Mental concentration is an essential ingredient for safe travel. Anyone easily distracted by what's going on around him or by the workings of his own mind is courting danger. An integral part of every mobility lesson is to remind the student to focus his attention on the ever-present demands of travel. The instructor discourages casual conversation when it interferes with concentration. He points out to the student the potential consequences of letting his mind wander. This is especially true while crossing, from the moment the student steps into a street until he reaches the opposite curb. If the student cannot or will not concentrate, even after training, street crossings should be postponed until maturation or a second round of training instills greater mental discipline.

The traveler should become aware not only of his responsibility for himself, but also of his indirect responsibility for the safety of others. An unthinking step might force a motorist to brake suddenly or veer out of control to avoid a collision. Tripping a passing pedestrian with a long cane could cause an unintented injury. The student must realize that his travel behavior could cause an accident.

Public Transportation

It is vital for the traveler to learn to use as many forms of public transportation as possible. This includes buses, subways, trains, and, if they exist in his community, trolley cars and ferry boats. Gaining access to public transportation widens the range of options for travel plans and constitutes a major component of outdoor mobility training. For many people, travel on public transportation is a visible sign of growing up, an integral part of normal, everyday life.

As a first step in training, the instructor familiarizes his student with each type of vehicle he is likely to use, in a manner similar to the orientation to new buildings described earlier. When feasible, the student explores an out-of-service bus, one parked at a company garage, for example, to get acquainted with the seating arrangement without being jostled by passengers or confronted by a harried bus driver. This also provides a good chance to discover where the coin box is located, what post to grab onto if the vehicle lurches, how to signal for the next stop and how to sit without blocking the aisle.

As an alternative to tracking down an empty bus, a mock-up construction of the forward section of a bus could be used: A couple of steps, the coin box and the driver's seat would suffice for practice in a classroom or rehabilitation center. The teacher might sit in the driver's seat, playing the role of the driver.

Boarding a bus requires the coordination of several actions simultaneously: Position oneself properly to hail the bus, display a special card for reduced fare, know the correct fare and deposit it into the coin box, request a transfer and place it securely in one's pocket, ask the driver to call out a certain street, and locate a seat within earshot of the driver. Each of these steps should be practiced separately or in small groupings, so the student does not feel overwhelmed or embarrassed when actually boarding a bus. People raised in the suburbs or in rural areas, where public transportation is not woven into the fabric of everyday life as much as in cities, may require extra attention while working on this phase of training. And the instructor must devise an ingenious plan for getting to public transportation.

A similar procedure may be followed for subways and trains. The student must be alerted to the grave danger of overstepping the edge of the platform in subway and train stations. In some cases, the danger may be greater for partially sighted travelers than for totally blind travelers, because indistinct visual clues, without confirmation by a probing cane, may be more deceptive than no visual clues at all.

The traveler needs to know about taxicabs: How to telephone for one, how to locate taxi stands and how to hail a passing cab. A person in a wheelchair should practice getting in and out of cabs until he can manage without undue strain or awkwardness. In Chicago cabs, it is easier for the wheelchair user to get into the front seat rather than the back seat because there is more room in the front seat. A law prohibiting passengers from sitting in the front seat of a cab may be waived if the traveler secures a letter of permission from the Chicago Department of Consumer Services.

During the past couple of decades, public transportation has become increasingly accessible to people who are disabled and those who are elderly, as advocacy and consumer groups lobbied in government hallways and demonstrated on city streets. They insist that public transportation is a civil right, that the system is subsidized by every taxpayer, and that it should be equally accessible and affordable.

As a direct result of sustained, highly publicized campaigns in various American cities, elevators were installed in selected subway stations and many city buses were fitted with special lifts that accommodate wheelchair users. In New York City, Los Angeles, the San Francisco Bay area, Denver, and Seattle, most buses are fitted with wheelchair lifts. Surveys indicate that the use of these devices does not delay bus operations. The incidence of mechanical breakdowns of wheelchair lifts had been fairly high, but as the market for lifts expands, the technology has improved, sharply reducing the number of breakdowns. Currently, the best record for minimizing the incidence of malfunctioning bus lifts is held by Seattle.

Kneeling buses, another type of modification, use a hydraulic suspension system that lowers the frame of the bus for easier boarding by wheelchair users. Due to the expensive price tag on kneeling buses, few of them are in service. Some communities are reluctant to purchase any lift-equipped buses or kneeling buses because of the limited number of riders who use them.

Faced with the high cost of making all public vehicles, stations, and terminals accessible for disabled and elderly people, transit authorities scrambled to devise less costly alternatives, which came to be called special services, as opposed to mainline services. This supplemental service, also called a paratransit system or dial-a-ride, consists of minibuses and vans equipped with lifts and collapsible ramps. It provides door-to-door transportation for people who qualify on the basis of physical inability to use regular buses and subways.

Paratransit systems are most extensively developed in cities where mainline buses and subways are not accessible to disabled people. In Chicago, for example, where city buses are currently not equipped with lifts, the paratransit system is highly developed. But transit authorities now realize that paratransit services are more expensive to operate than making mainline service accessible. Some advocates of full access recommend a mixture of paratransit and mainline services, rather than total reliance on one system to the exclusion of the other.

Private taxicabs play a role in some paratransit systems. Rather than paying full fare, the eligible rider pays only the cost of a one-way trip on public transportation. The remainder of the cost is borne by the local transit authority, which is subsidized by state and federal funds. In Boston, where the paratransit system is called Dial-a-Ride, a one-way fare costs 60 cents. In New York, after paying a 5 dollar registration fee, a one-way ride costs 6 dollars. Since about 50 percent of transportation-disabled people are elderly with lower incomes, an affordable and accessible transportation system is a significant concern for a growing percentage of the population.

To become eligible for a Special Services Card in Chicago, the applicant must obtain written confirmation from a physician certifying that the individual is unable to climb the three standard-size steps needed to board a coach, or is both blind and deaf. The applicant must also furnish a photograph of himself or herself, which is then affixed to the card for easy identification. Once declared eligible, the rider calls a central number to reserve a ride 24 hours prior to his scheduled trip. A minibus arrives at his home and whisks him to his destination. The return trip must likewise be arranged in advance.

Every day, more than a thousand Chicagoans take advantage of this service. The major problem is that thousands more would like to use it, but are turned away because this door-to-door service can satisfy the travel needs of only a portion of those who need it. The others are compelled to pay for cabs, rely on friends, or remain at home.

The adolescent student who is retarded tires of riding the yellow school bus (often dubbed the "baby bus") and yearns to ride on public transportation, just like everyone else. After successfully completing his first bus trip alone, the student beams with pride and feels, perhaps for the first time, like an adult. This joy is shared by his parents, who may rekindle hopes for their youngster's future, and by peers who respect and admire this visible badge of long-awaited maturity.

When someone in a wheelchair travels by plane, he can expect two courtesies: The privilege of boarding ahead of other passengers and, once inside the aircraft, the transfer to a specially-designed wheelchair, narrow enough to fit through the aisle. Mobile chairs are available on some widebodied planes so physically disabled people can move more easily from their seats to lavatories, some of which are fitted with support bars. In certain aisle seats, armrests can be raised so the passenger can slide from his seat to a mobile chair. First class seats are the easiest to reach, but most people travel coach, so the forward seats in the coach section are the most convenient.

During the past decade a controversy surfaced regarding the right of blind people to sit wherever they choose on airplanes. Some airline officials demand that blind passengers sit next to an emergency exit for easier evacuation. Officials of other airlines prohibit blind passengers from sitting next to emergency exits, because they supposedly would hinder evacuation of other passengers during an emergency.

In the past several years, dozens of blind passengers have been arrested and many others have been forcibly removed from planes in seating disputes. Some groups of blind people regard this requirement as unnecessary and demeaning. They are testing the validity of seating regulations in the courts, seeking to have them voided as discriminatory against blind passengers. This unresolved issue continues to boil with no immediate solution in sight.

Driver Education

Driving your own car, pickup truck, or van is a cherished goal for most Americans, and people with disabilities are no exceptions. Many disabled people can reach this key to freedom on their own, while others must receive proper training, and install adaptive devices in their vehicles.

Some rehabilitation centers train people with paraplegia and quadriplegia to drive cars and vans equipped with hydraulic hand controls that reduce the amount of physical strength needed for steering and braking. Many students are strong enough to drive with ordinary power steering and power brakes. If the driver's left foot is stronger than his right, an adapter can be installed which enables the driver to brake and accelerate with his left foot. Some vans contain collapsible ramps, so wheelchairs can be rolled in and out.

After earning a driver's license, people with disabilities are as free as anyone else to drive. If a driver must use hand controls, that restriction would be noted on his driver's license. (A few physically disabled adventurers go one step further. They take flying lessons, earn a pilot's license and pilot a private plane. One determined wheelchair user took up sky diving, solving the landing problem by descending into a body of water.)

Parking inconveniences are reduced by spaces reserved for disabled drivers. These spaces are designated by signs with the international symbol for the disabled: A white line drawing of a wheelchair on a blue background. The driver displays a state-issued card on the dashboard, or uses a special license plate which entitles the driver to park in spaces reserved for disabled people. These parking regulations have increasingly been enforced, but violators continue to disregard them. Some municipalities hire disabled people to issue parking tickets, with fines of up to 50 dollars.

Drivers with disabilities do not always escape the dreaded parking ticket because wide discrepancies in parking regulations create confusion. One state might not honor another state's method of identification or a police officer might not recognize an out-of-state designation for a disabled motorist. The driver may be uncertain about what parking privileges he is entitled to after leaving his home state. Adding to the confusion is a wide variation in the definition of a disabled driver.

Fifteen states honor disabled designations from all states, while 34 others have entered into agreements with specific states. The Federal Highway Administration is developing a model state law that would include uniform disability designations on cars and mutual recognition among the states of any variations in how a disabled driver is identified. Still to be worked out are a standard definition of disability and a standard symbol for a disabled motorist.

As driver education courses proliferate in American high schools, many states require that all students, including those with disabilities, enroll in a driver theory course. Those who cannot learn to drive get acquainted with traffic laws which govern motorists. Blind students learn about the rights of pedestrians, even though driving is out of the question for them. It is important for them to know that a state motor vehicle law requires motorists to yield the right of way to blind people carrying white canes or using guide dogs while crossing streets.

Although legally blind people are not eligible to drive, those with visual acuity above legal blindness do drive, and some of them benefit by using bioptic telescopic lenses. The driver looks through the lower portion of regular glasses to view near objects, and then shifts his vision to telescopic lenses in the upper part to focus on distant features. These visual aids can make the difference between being able to drive safely or not.

Some driver education courses are adapted to the needs of students who are mildly and moderately retarded, using a gradual progression of instructional steps and appropriate modifications. Not every student succeeds, but every youngster should be given the opportunity to participate in the classroom phase. Some students enroll in an adaptive program for the classroom phase, where simulators are used, and then participate in the regular, on-the-road driving phase. Continuous monitoring of the student's driving and parental involvement are important elements of these courses.

Elderly people are reluctant to give up their lifelong habit of driving because they love the sense of independence it provides. Those living in rural areas are even more reluctant to stop driving than city-dwellers because they have fewer transportation options. Losing the ability to drive severely alters their lifestyle. This increases the risk of deterioration in physical functioning; depression may surface or a downbeat mood may become aggravated.

Many elderly drivers undergo physiological changes that impair driving ability: Slowed reflexes, heart disease, weakened muscles, and visual inability to cope with glare. Diminished depth perception makes it harder to judge the speed of oncoming cars and loss of peripheral vision makes cars seem to come out of nowhere. It becomes more difficult to look left and right due to arthritis or bursitis. The unexpected side-effects of medications can add to the problem. Arthritis medication, for example, could cause drowsiness.

Some elderly drivers become progressively more fearful. Will their car break down while driving at night, exposing them to danger from passing thugs? Even if fears and worries don't terminate driving, they may restrict personal mobility by reducing the range of driving.

Family members encourage elderly drivers to take extra safety precautions. They advise them to stop driving at night and to drive on roads best suited for their abilities. They should share driving time with other people, such as a spouse. Many women discover after it's too late that they are unable to travel independently after their husbands die. Ideally, they would learn to drive earlier in life and find out about senior ride programs.

As an incentive to encourage driver vigilance, insurance companies offer discounts for attendance at refresher courses, many of which are offered at community colleges. The American Association of Retired Persons also organizes courses in every state for drivers over 50. Students are given practical suggestions such as how to map out an alternate route if turnpike traffic becomes congested or moves too fast for comfort. They are cautioned against failing to yield the right of way, making improper left turns or incorrect lane changes, and passing other vehicles improperly.

Older drivers must undergo a relicensing procedure at a specified age. Some states restrict the renewal of licenses for drivers 65 and over, and thirteen states require special tests. A physical exam is required in Louisiana after age 75, and a road test is necessary in Illinois after age 69.

On the positive side, thousands of elderly people increase their mobility after retirement. They joyfully hop into their recreational vehicles and motor homes (not mobile homes, which can't be driven). They head for the long, winding road, logging more miles each year than ever before, as family and financial concerns become less pressing. They enjoy socializing at campgrounds and parks. They indulge a wanderlust that sat dormant for years, choosing travel, in whatever form, as the best way to fill their retirement with happiness.

Shopping

Shopping is just as important in the life of a disabled person as it is for anyone else. The corner grocery, a drug store, a record shop, a department store—access to all these businesses is crucial for a disabled person who values independence.

The traveler must know how to get to these shops and what to do once inside. He draws on outdoor mobility skills while going to the store and indoor mobility skills within the store. Social skills come into play as he turns to a salesclerk for information or assistance. Relevant complementary skills include handling money, writing a check, or using a credit card.

The student absorbs basic information while in a grocery store, such as where the produce department is located and what items are displayed there. He discovers the relative prices of various items, indirectly learning the value of money. The student must make certain judgments, such as buying no more groceries than he can comfortably carry home. These skills can't be learned all at once. They must be acquired one by one over a reasonable period.

The shopping segment of mobility training begins with exposure to small, uncrowded stores, preferably in the student's home neighborhood. The instructor acquaints the student with the layout of the entire store and the variety of merchandise sold there. After telling the student what he expects him to do in the store, he assists only as necessary. On subsequent trips, the instructor observes from an inconspicuous place in the store. Finally, the student enters the store alone, makes a purchase and reports afterward on how things went.

This procedure is repeated in various stores, culminating in the complexities of a department store, if one exists in the community. If not, the largest store in town serves as the final step. Orientation to a shopping mall is a valuable addition to this phase of training: What is the physical arrangement of the mall? What kinds of stores are located there? Where in the mall can a shopper get additional information? One lesson might be devoted to window-shopping, so the student learns to surmise from window displays the range of merchandise sold in each store.

Larger stores and shopping malls often provide the student's first encounter with escalators or elevators, as well as revolving doors. Observing the student's abilities, the instructor judges whether to encourage him to use escalators, elevators and revolving doors unassisted or advise him to use them only with suitable assistance. The instructor might suggest that the student avoid them completely.

Eating Out

Feeling comfortable while eating out—at a hot dog stand or in a fine restaurant—is a well-established goal in mobility training. Some people with disabilities have little experience eating out. Perhaps they avoid doing so because of feeling awkward or out of place. In a wide variety of eating places, the student learns during mobility lessons, not only the mechanics of purchasing food, but also how to relax and enjoy dining in public, eventually shedding self-consciousness and resistance. The instructor's easygoing manner serves as a model for the student to emulate.

Trips to eateries are often arranged as interludes during mobility lessons that focus on other objectives. While teaching a downtown route, for example, the instructor decides that both of them could use a break, so they enter a coffee shop. On the first visit, the instructor orders the beverages and, if the student is blind, describes prominent features of the shop's interior. On return visits, the student takes the reins and purchases his own beverage.

In a similar way, the student masters dining at other kinds of eating places: He waits his turn in line at a fast-food counter, selects his favorite dishes in a cafeteria, tells a waiter what food he wants to order in a restaurant, pays the bill, and leaves a tip. The fledgling customer eventually gains enough confidence to send back to the kitchen any food not cooked to his satisfaction. Care should be taken in a restaurant to ensure that the waiter addresses the disabled person directly and not his companion with the question: "What does he want?"

Braille menus are available in some restaurants for blind customers who want to find out the selections for themselves. Hard-of-hearing students are advised to sit away from the kitchen and cash register, so the noise coming from these places will not interfere with conversation. If a student is too shy to request a seat in a particular section, the mobility instructor might build a lesson around coaxing the student to assert himself in an appropriate way.

Chapter 4

SOCIAL AND COMPLEMENTARY SKILLS

SOCIAL SKILLS

As the desire and ability to travel increase, so does the necessity of interacting with other people. Conversing with a guide or companion, telling a salesperson what one wants, asking the bus driver for a transfer —interpersonal contacts are a natural and unavoidable feature of the mobility landscape. Gaining an understanding of social competencies and obligations goes hand in hand with developing mobility skills. Both sets of skills overlap and reinforce each other.

For some people, talking with others is as easy as taking a sip of water. But for those with lingering immaturity or social awkwardness, contact with the public may seem as difficult as pushing a boulder up a steep hill. It is to the student's advantage to feel comfortable with the normal give-and-take that binds people together, to become adept enough at verbal exchanges to hold up his end of conversations, to interact with others in socially acceptable ways. It also helps for the student to become aware of the impact of the nonverbal signals, body language, and facial expressions that can be as important for communication as verbal exchanges. Social maturity, then, in its practical, applied sense, becomes an integral part of mobility training. The instructor organizes lessons that prompt his students to initiate conversations and make inquiries, as interaction with the public increases.

Some examples of social skills are: Mastering the basic rules of courtesy, exchanging friendly greetings, remembering to say please and thank you, being reasonably tolerant and patient with other people's idiosyncracies, showing respect and consideration for the needs of others, tactfully requesting, accepting, or declining assistance. But being polite might be difficult for an individual who wants so badly to reclaim his independence that he angrily refuses any offer of assistance.

Other examples of social skills are controlling the swing of one's cane so it doesn't trip anyone, keeping one's feet and cane out of aisles, maneuvering a wheelchair without interfering with passersby, and on a day wet with rain or snow, wiping one's feet (or wheels) before entering someone's home.

Social acceptability is influenced by the way we dress, talk, and act, by our personal habits of grooming and hygiene. An amiable smile, friendly eye contact, a pleasant appearance, and age-appropriate behavior empower the traveler to achieve his goals with greater ease, assurance, and enjoyment.

Those who are walled off by social isolation become passive and lose the spunk needed to reach out to other people. They simply wait for others to come to them. Overcoming passivity becomes a goal in the mobility process as the instructor encourages each student to increase contact with the public. He urges each student to speak clearly and ask questions that will elicit the most useful answers.

A deaf person can write down questions and receive written responses, if no other means of communication are effective. With experience, the student realizes that requesting appropriate help is not a threat to his pride or independence. With a sense of relief, he discovers that he doesn't have to prove himself repeatedly to others.

The knack of putting others at ease is a valuable asset for anyone. But this talent is especially useful when a disabled person encounters someone uneasy about face-to-face contact with a disabled person. The more comfortable the disabled person feels about himself (and about his disability), the more readily he can calm the concerns of new acquaintances. The more he relaxes, the more he can be appreciated as a unique individual with assets and faults like everyone else. But first the person must desensitize himself regarding his own disability, a process that may require considerable time, depending on the strength of his motivation.

Anger, resentment, and self-pity are strong emotions that can erect barriers and drive people away. As the grip of negative emotions loosens, if in fact they exist, the student stands a better chance to normalize relations with fellow human beings.

The disabled person learns that helping other people is a two-way street. In certain situations, he assists others as well as being helped by them. In a familiar place, for instance, he gives clear directions to someone who is lost. A person with an electric wheelchair helps to start a stranded motorist's car by hooking starter cables to the battery on his wheelchair.

A sense of humor, even if it's self-deprecating, dispells social tensions.

Sharing a laugh is a time-honored way to forge bonds between people. (As Victor Borge says, "The shortest distance between two people is a good laugh.") Laughing at yourself, getting in touch with the lighter side of one's personality and life in general, furnishes welcome relief for all concerned. As the student takes himself less seriously, he becomes more approachable by other people, even in casual contacts.

A good sense of humor means not only creating amusing sidelights, but also appreciating humor generated by others. The God-given capacity to laugh should be nurtured and kept alive, and regarded as a precious resource in life's journey. At the very least, a smile beats a frown every time.

Humor often rears its curly head in mobility situations, if you know where to look and how to react when you find it. The experienced instructor welcomes humor and prods it along. The instructor and student share a good laugh recalling a stranger who insisted on escorting the student three blocks to a store, even though the student had asked one simple question about the name of a street. Each trip is an adventure, so everyone involved might as well share some fun along the way.

Speech disabilities, deviations from normal speech noticeable enough to draw unfavorable attention to the speaker, interfere with the smooth flow of communication. They run the gamut from a slight lisp to total inability to speak. Speaking too softly to be understood is a common problem, which might stem from shyness, uncertainty, or inexperience, or possibly a physical dysfunction. Weak vocal projection and lack of clear articulation warrant therapeutic attention because they interfere with the student's ability to secure help and make satisfying personal contacts.

The mobility instructor encourages the student to speak clearly during lessons whenever contact is made with other people, including conversations with the instructor. He coaches the student on such voice qualities as tone and pitch, and on the proper distance between people when they talk to each other.

A disabled person may be approached by a stranger who wants to assist but is unsure about how to do so. The disabled person must express clearly what help he wants and the best manner of providing it. When someone grabs a blind person's arm and pushes him forward, the blind person might well say, "Please let me hold your arm until we get across the street." Someone wanting to assist a wheelchair user negotiate a curb may need specific directions about how to accomplish that feat safely.

Communication skills and mobility skills are tightly interwoven; they are inseparable.

A person with his larynx removed learns to use his mechanical voice box in public without embarrassment. The instructor encourages a cerebral palsied student to use his voice as best he can and to persevere in trying to be understood. If these and other speech problems such as stuttering persist, referral to a speech therapist would be advisable.

A young blind girl speaks clearly and intelligently, but has a habit of tilting her head downward while talking. When asked why, she confides, "Nobody wants to see my funny eyes." The instructor, in cooperation with her teacher and parents, encourages her to shine her face as well as her words on other people whenever she talks with them. When someone speaks to her, the instructor points out, she should face the speaker, as a courtesy and as a way of strengthening contact with the other person.

When a disabled person accompanied by a companion encounters someone, that third person often addresses the companion, even regarding something that directly concerns the disabled person. As a man walking with a cane for support and his wife enter an art museum, an attendant asks the woman, "Does he need a wheelchair?" Such discourtesy, even though unintentional, irritates and chips away self-esteem. It treats the disabled person as though he were a child, or worse yet, a nonperson.

Personal affronts can be countered. A wheelchair rider and his friend, for example, enter a men's clothing store to purchase a necktie. As they approach the salesperson, he automatically makes eye contact with the person pushing the wheelchair and asks, "Can I help you?" Again, unintentionally, the person in the wheelchair is relegated to the role of an observer or a second-class citizen. If, however, by prior agreement, the companion averts his eyes, ignoring the clerk, the disabled person has a better chance to assert himself as the customer, and as a worthwhile human being who can communicate directly with other people.

Eye level influences this situation. The nondisabled person stands at about the same height as the salesclerk, but the wheelchair user must look up and the salesperson must look down to make eye contact. While not meaning to treat the wheelchair user as a child, the wheelchair user's eye level is actually at the same height as a child's eye level.

Role-playing exercises help untangle social dilemmas. The necktie scene could be reenacted in any room by the wheelchair user and two other people, one playing the role of the companion, the other the insensitive clerk. The disabled person then has ample opportunity to choose the right words and tone of voice to convey his message: "I'm looking for a necktie; would you please show me your selection?" After each enactment, observers share their perception of the disabled person's actions and suggest constructive changes, such as: make eye contact sooner, a little smile wouldn't hurt, speak a little louder so the clerk understands you the first time you say something, and say it like you mean it. Positive feedback furnishes food for growth and understanding. One cautionary note on role-playing exercises: They should be used as preparation for real situations, not as a substitute for them.

In a similar way, a classroom could be converted into an imaginary candy store where a retarded student purchases a chocolate bar from the teacher, who poses as the clerk. In this easy-going environment, the student takes time to speak clearly, count his change, put the coins in a safe place, say thank you, and remember to take the candy bar. Variations of this exercise are repeated until the student's progress signals that he's ready for the real thing.

Deaf people and workers with the deaf have debated for decades about the most effective and proper method of communication. One question is whether deaf and hearing impaired people should use American Sign Language, which is a gestural language that relies on the hands, face, head, body, posture and use of the space in front of the body to convey information. Or should they use spoken speech and lipreading? This issue has not been resolved, but a significant trend in the past couple of decades has been toward a concept known as "Total Communication." An adherent of this approach uses all possible means of communication, sometimes simultaneously, each method reinforcing the meaning of the others to project one's message. He uses sign language, fingerspelling, lip movements, gestures, and facial and bodily movements to express himself. If further clarification is needed, he writes his message on a piece of paper. A great number of deaf people use their voices while communicating, but some remain silent if they think their speech is difficult to understand, or if they feel they have inappropriate pitch or volume control. Some learn to understand spoken language by reading lips, but this is an extremely difficult skill to master, since less than 30 percent of all speech sounds is visible on the lips.

Hearing impaired people who are afraid of being misunderstood or appearing foolish resist communicating with hearing people. It is a special talent to feel comfortable with hearing people who do not understand sign language. The instructor incorporates exercises into mobility lessons that bolster the ability of hearing impaired students to communicate with the hearing public, using whatever methods are effective. These exercises may become the focal point of mobility training.

Some hearing impaired people can be identified by their hearing aid. But deafness is usually a subtle, often invisible disability. Onlookers might mistakenly perceive a deaf person's problem as stemming from other causes, such as inattention, rudeness, or aloofness. It takes strong personal resolve by the deaf person to convey to hearing people that he cannot hear. Not everyone can or wants to do that, because it may seem easier to get by without exposing one's disability, to create the impression of being just like everyone else, or to avoid making contact with hearing people.

The same psychological dynamic influences partially sighted people who prefer to conceal their impairment. But it is an asset to be open about one's disability and to speak about it directly. This openness promotes understanding and acceptance among acquaintances. When a partially sighted person brings his eyes close to a page to read it, or when a hearing impaired person stands unusually close to another person to hear better, informed acquaintances will not view these practical adjustment as bizarre behavior. A person who uses a wheelchair only occasionally will not feel awkward when he stands up if people understand his special needs.

Like any other relationship, contact between disabled and nondisabled people is a two-way street in which tact and common sense are desirable from both sides. Disabled people are as different from one another as those without disabilities; they have the same range of personality traits as nondisabled people do. There are certain things a disabled person cannot do easily or at all.

Here are some general pointers that may be useful when interacting with a disabled person:

(1) When meeting a blind person, it is not necessary to talk louder than usual. If a person loses his sight it does not mean that he also loses his sense of hearing. Nor can you assume that he is helpless, gifted, hard-of-hearing or an accomplished musician.

(2) Take a little more initiative than usual and begin by making your presence known with a casual hello or other appropriate greeting. Even if you have met the person before, avoid playing games like, "Guess who I am?" It is best to identify yourself right away. The blind person who

wants to shake hands with you may make only a small gesture, moving his hand slightly upward from his side because he doesn't know exactly where your hand is or whether you wish to shake hands. If you see his hand make such a movement, reach for it, even though it requires you to go more than half way.

(3) If you wonder whether a blind person needs your help, or anyone else for that matter, the best idea is to ask if he would like some assistance, in a calm, matter-of-fact way that is not patronizing or maudlin. If your offer is turned down, don't insist on helping anyhow. You should assume that the blind person knows his own mind. If your offer is accepted, don't provide any more help than is necessary.

(4) When leading a blind person, control your natural impulse to grab his arm and push him ahead of you. The blind person will have a greater sense of security and direction if he holds on to your arm just above the elbow. You take the initiative by asking him to put his hand there and, at the same time, placing his hand just above your elbow with your free hand. Walk slightly ahead of your partner, at a pace that feels comfortable to both of you.

(5) Before pushing a person in a wheelchair, always ask permission. An unexpected push could cause the person to tumble out of the chair or otherwise upset him. The wheelchair is an extension of that person, a part of his bodily space and should be treated accordingly. Be careful when pushing it so you don't cause him to topple forward out of the chair. When going up or down curbs, there is no reliable rule other than listening to the directions offered by the wheelchair user.

(6) When speaking to a wheelchair user for more than a few minutes, place yourself on the same plane by sitting or squatting. This puts both of you on an equal footing, and relieves his neck muscles from the strain of looking up. Ask if he wants to transfer out of his wheelchair to some other place. If he does transfer out of his wheelchair, don't move his wheelchair out of reach, because he may want to transfer back to it.

COMPLEMENTARY SKILLS

It takes practice for a student to follow a set of directions such as this: "Start on the northwest corner of State and Monroe; travel west on the south side of Monroe for two blocks until you reach Clark Street; then turn south and locate a drug store at 106 South Clark Street." Getting on top of this mental game is an integral part of mobility training and falls within the fourth major category of mobility training: Complementary Skills.

Some examples of these miscellaneous skills are reading street signs and bus signs, and understanding compass points as they relate to gaining one's bearings. Since the use of compass points can be confusing for anyone, a sizeable number of students cannot be expected to benefit significantly from exercises to improve this particular skill. Other examples of complementary skills are seeking facts about public transportation routes, and gathering relevant details for planning a trip. The ability to elicit pertinent information is a key to successful planning; knowing what to do when lost is the key to regaining one's confidence.

A partially sighted student learns to use a low-vision aid: a hand-held, miniature telescope with strong powers of magnification that enhances vision, enabling him to gain information from distant objects. The instructor guides the student's use of the distance aid by directing him to read a bus sign or spot the number on the front of a house or recognize warning signals, such as flashing red lights. The student's ability to use an optical aid is strengthened through repeated use during mobility lessons.

The student might feel self-conscious when first holding an aid to his eye while in public view, but as appreciation of the aid's value grows, embarrassment recedes, as does his need to rely on other people for information and assistance. For the student who squints while watching for the traffic light to change on a bright, sunny day, the instructor might recommend the use of sunglasses.

Sensory training for blind students focuses on the senses of hearing, touch, and smell. The instructor draws the student's attention to the useful bits of information that sensory cues can provide. He points out how they help to compensate for the loss of visual cues. The instructor asks the student, for example, to stand on a street corner and interpret various traffic sounds and patterns. In this way, the student learns to use the traffic in a positive way, rather than regarding it solely as a source of danger.

The instructor explains the value of echolocation, which means judging the distance between a traveler and some object by listening to variations in the pitch of echoing sounds. Some blind travelers wear taps on their heels or snap their fingers when approaching an object to detect changes in pitch, which goes up as he approaches an object. Echolocation also enables a blind traveler to walk in a straight line parallel to a wall or a row of buildings by listening to sound variations along the wall. This is the same principle used in radar, and, in a more natural realm, by bats, as they instinctively home in on even miniscule objects in total darkness.

Blind students learn to be more sensitive to changes in air pressure, which indicates whether a door is open or where two hallways intersect. The instructor might ask the student to walk along a sidewalk and stop in front of a bakery, identifying the store solely on the basis of the inviting aroma wafting through the air. Skillful use of remaining senses helps students decipher otherwise hidden messages in the environment, messages that guide safe passage through a jumble of sensory signals.

It is commonly believed that blind people automatically develop more acute senses by virtue of their blindness, that they miraculously sprout special talents such as an exceptional musical ability. This simply is not true. It is a myth perpetuated by people with a lively imagination but little if any direct contact with blind people. Some people with disabilities cultivate their senses and talents out of choice or necessity, through practice and determination. But their talents were not miraculously bestowed on them. They were earned the old-fashioned way, through hard work, just as anyone else achieves a coveted goal.

Concept development enables a blind student to create mental images that correspond reasonably well to objects and their relationship in his environment. Particularly for a congenitally blind student, concept development bridges gaps in his perception and understanding of his surroundings. What does it mean to be in back of something, in front of it or beside it? To move sideways? To make a U turn? To turn around completely? Where is the back of his knee, the front of his neck? How does a square differ from a triangle or a circle? What is the usual shape of a car or truck? What does the color red signify to sighted people? What's the difference between an intersection with two-way stop signs and one with four-way stop signs? What's the difference between parallel and perpendicular lines of traffic?

It is important to learn the basic units of measurement: inch, foot, yard, and mile, along with some knowledge about the metric system. On a larger scale, what is meant by a business district, a city, a county, a state, a country, a continent? The student needs to know the units of time, such as second, minute, and hour, as well as the concept of yesterday, today, and tomorrow. He needs to understand the two scales used for measuring temperature: Celsius and Fahrenheit.

Being able to estimate time and distance are worthwhile skills to develop. The student learns to estimate how long a round trip will take from one point to another and approximately how many miles will be covered. How much time does it take to walk a mile, or to drive in a car for 100 miles? Mental exercises such as these could be combined with the concept of punctuality: Why is it important for the traveler to arrive on time for an appointment?

A blind child's conception of what a grandfather clock looks like is aided by the simple act of lifting him up, so he can explore with his own hands the top part of the clock. Rather than merely describing a stop sign, have him explore it. This hands-on approach is the most effective way to teach people with visual impairments. There are limits, however, such as the question of whether blind people should be encouraged to touch other people's faces to form an impression of their features. Some believe that this is an invasion of other people's privacy. The answer to this question is best left to the discretion of parents and teachers.

Some art museums, conscious of the needs of blind people, mount exhibitions that can be touched, such as a collection of sturdy sculptures. A huge Calder sculpture standing in front of the Dirksen Federal Building in Chicago can be explored in its entirety by blind people using a scale model, which is housed in the lobby of that building. Guided tours of the Smithsonian Museum and the nation's Capitol are available with sign language interpreters for the enjoyment of deaf people. Some museums provide closed captions on audio-visual displays.

A New York artist, Willa Shalit, specializes in making masks of public personalities. Collections of these masks, called life-cast sculptures, have been exhibited at centers in New York so blind people can explore the infinite variety of expressions on people's faces, including some of America's celebrities.

A person in a wheelchair feels more secure about planning and making a trip if he determines beforehand what buildings are relatively easy to enter, what hotels are accessible, and what travel tours accommodate people in wheelchairs. He needs to know if there is a level or ramped entrance or low steps and whether parking is available nearby. Is there a restaurant on the premises with a level access? He can glean some of this information from access guides and handbooks for disabled people, which are available in most major cities.

In San Francisco, for example, the Mayor's Council on Disabilities Concerns published a pamphlet recently that contains useful information about churches, synagogues, hotels, motels, museums, restaurants, and shopping centers. The pamphlet indicates whether restrooms are accessible to wheelchair users and whether an elevator is available in buildings that have more than one story.

In addition to access guides, the traveler should also know what information he can expect from Traveler's Aid or a local travel agency. Some travel agencies specialize in booking trips for disabled people, their staff being knowledgeable, experienced, and understanding about the need for special accommodations.

For those interested in details about access in National Parks, books and pamphlets are now available that describe not only barrier-free accommodations, but also the grade and surface of roads and pathways, the availability of telecommunication devices and the proximity of hospitals and medical support services. They also note the location of veterinarians who can care for guide dogs.

Careful planning takes some of the chanciness out of any trip. Planning not only minimizes travel problems, it is a large part of the fun of traveling. The sensible traveler writes or calls ahead of time to a hotel, specifying his personal requirements and confirms reservations after they have been made. Someone in a wheelchair learns by experience to reserve a seat on the aisle when attending the theatre. At the end of an athletic contest, he waits patiently in his seat until the bulk of the crowd has exited. Or, if it's not a cliffhanger, he might beat the crowd by leaving before the end of the game.

Travel by a retarded student is eased by building basic reading skills, which help him to comprehend key travel-related terms, such as exit, do not enter, danger, walk, don't walk, one-way street, taxi stand, bus stop, and subway. It is useful for any traveler to understand the meaning of such colloquial expressions as "bumper to bumper" and "traffic jam." What is the meaning of the joke that labels the major expressway leading into a city as the world's longest parking lot? The ability to recognize numbers, such as 93rd Street, is also important. Complementary skills spell the difference between getting there and getting lost, and they increase a traveler's sense of being in control.

If Elm Street is an important landmark on a route, but the student cannot reliably read the street sign, he might carry a card with Elm Street written on it. The student could then confirm the name by matching the card with the street sign. Such cards could be used with any important name or number along the route. They might also serve to jog the student's memory about which street or address he was searching for.

Money management is an essential skill that no traveler can afford to neglect. The student should be able to identify each coin and bill up to at least twenty dollars. For practice, the instructor gives the student a handful of mixed coins and asks him to return 55 cents. Or the student pretends that he is buying a 35 cent candy bar. After giving the instructor one dollar, how much change can he expect? The student should learn how to prevent being short-changed in a store by concentrating on the transaction. Before the student makes a trip into the city on public transportation, he should add up all the fares he must pay, so he will know in advance the total cost of the trip. The student should learn what a sales tax is and how it is calculated, so the total cost of his purchases makes more sense.

It is equally important to guard against losing money by keeping it in a safe place. Making correct change, counting money accurately, safeguarding money—these travel-related skills deserve attention from the student and from those who educate him.

Many blind people devise a personal system for keeping track of coins and bills. One such system calls for a wallet that is divided lengthwise into two sections. The blind person places one dollar bills in one section and five dollar bills in the other. He identifies ten dollar bills by folding them in half and twenty dollar bills by folding them four times. If he keeps pennies in a separate pocket, the other coins are fairly easy to distinguish from one another.

Students learn to select appropriate clothing and footwear after listening to weather reports on television or radio, or by reading the forecast in a newspaper. The teacher may arrange simple exercises, such as reading aloud the latest weather prediction and then quizzing her class on what specific articles of clothing they would choose for comfort and protection under the conditions described.

Mobility lessons are usually conducted in all types of the weather, so the student gets used to the idea that mobility is not merely a pleasant outing on a day when the sun shines. Fostering this habit teaches the student how to adjust in terms of clothing choice, as well as cane and wheelchair techniques. This practice prepares the student for the world of work, where employees (and employers) are expected on the job regardless of weather conditions.

Another example of complementary skills is the effective use of the telephone. The student learns how to locate pay phones, to dial for information, to contact the operator and dial an emergency number. The instructor advises him to carry in a safe place the telephone numbers of one or two persons who would assist him if he got lost or an emergency arose. He should carry enough change to make at least one phone call. He learns that some shopping can be accomplished by telephone, a convenience which is especially valuable during inclement weather or illness. When calling a disabled person, it is considerate to allow a few extra rings before hanging up, because it might take him longer to answer the phone.

Telecommunication devices for the deaf (TDD) enabled deaf people to communicate by telephone. The TDD looks like a typewriter with a telephone attached to it. A deaf person types a message which is then transmitted over regular telephone lines to a party with similar equipment. The message is then converted back to print, which the deaf person receiving the call can read on his TDD. Deaf people with a limited amount of hearing, called residual hearing, benefit from a telephone amplifier.

The ability to read and understand maps is a valuable asset for anyone who travels. Reading maps is a challenge that actively engages the student's mental powers and helps him chart the best route through unfamiliar territory. The instructor begins by drawing simple maps of the student's school and home neighborhoods, including alley ways. Later, the instructor shifts to printed maps of the city, marking important landmarks, such as appropriate community agencies the student would be likely to visit on personal business.

With a little prompting, students can draw their own maps of various neighborhoods to demonstrate their retention of street names and understanding of street patterns. Partially sighted students benefit by using pencils with heavy points or pens with broad tips that produce dark, thick lines. Blind students use special paper with the texture of cellophane that produces a raised line when drawn on with a metal point. The student can then "read" the map by touch.

Map orientation should include mental games based on the compass points, such as: What major street runs three blocks northeast of the school? The instructor designates one wall of a classroom as the north wall, another the south, the east and the west wall, so students become familiar with compass relationships in their daily routines. Can the student locate the northeast corner of the room?

An occupational therapist working with a stroke patient who is about to reenter the community, gives him a map so he can mark his chosen route with a red pencil for easy reference.

The instructor explains the local numbering system used for addresses. Are even numbers assigned to the north side of the street or the south side? Are odd numbers on the west or east side of the street? How many blocks would you expect to walk to get from 400 Maple Street to 800 Maple Street? This explanation should also include the indoor numbering system: rooms on the first floor are in the 100s, and the 200s are located on the second floor, and so on.

A three dimensional model of an intersection, complete with toy cars and trucks, helps students understand traffic flow, how cars change lanes and the function of stop signs and traffic lights.

Working with the Iowa State Department of Education several years ago, Bruce McClanahan designed a computer program for partially sighted students to sharpen their directional skills. A computer, equipped with synthetic speech, gives the student such directions as: "Walk three blocks south on Oak Street and two blocks west on Grove." Then it asks: "At what intersection have you arrived?" To find the answer, the student analyzes a large-print map which comes with the program. After selecting an answer to each multiple choice question on the computer screen, the computer voice informs the student immediately whether his answer is correct or not. Several different types of programs using variations of this directional theme are available.

Many of the complementary skills described can be taught under simulated conditions, for the sake of convenience. Some rehabilitation hospitals, for example, bring parts of the outside world into the confines of the hospital by constructing or installing a turnstile, a curb, a restaurant, a grocery store, a small car or the forward section of a bus. For some patients, practice with realistic props eases the transition from hospital back to normal life, and may spell the difference between returning to their own home or entering a nursing home.

Chapter 5

PRINCIPLES OF MOBILITY TRAINING

There is a temptation to regard mobility training as a professional discipline so different from other disciplines that existing knowledge from allied fields cannot be selectively borrowed and applied. This misconception stems largely from the fact that mobility training is a relatively young profession, a therapeutic discipline unfamiliar to most people, and one which addresses the needs of a relatively small number of students.

In actual practice, however, mobility training is more similar to other teaching strategies than it is unique. Similarities are especially striking with regard to the underlying teaching principles, which closely resemble those governing most other aspects of special education and rehabilitation.

The following general principles do not apply exclusively to mobility training, but they are especially relevant to that discipline.

THE WORKING RELATIONSHIP BETWEEN INSTRUCTOR AND STUDENT

The crucial importance of a good working relationship between instructor and student cannot be overstated. This relationship, which rests on the blending of two personalities in a working partnership, is the key ingredient of effective training. It influences, as much as any other single factor, the ease with which travel techniques are learned and the ultimate outcome of training.

The successful instructor is warm and accepting, even when prodding the student to higher levels of independence. He is friendly, yet reserved enough to control the direction of the relationship. He is able to be firm, even though he feels empathy for his students' struggle to surmount obstacles. His contacts with students are characterized by a caring, sensitive manner, and the skillful application of mobility know-how. He knows that a reassuring touch calms students when circumstances become unsettling.

The instructor realizes that an upbeat, cheerful manner makes lessons feel more like playing a game than like trudging through a therapeutic but tiresome exercise. Like a tightrope walker, he adeptly walks the line between being casual and friendly and being firm and businesslike. He makes corrections in a positive way, so students perceive his remarks as constructive criticism.

The alert instructor always looks for signs that the student is ready to move ahead. If the instructor assigns advanced mobility tasks prematurely, before the student is equipped to deal with them, physical injury may result or the student's emotions may get bruised, leaving him dispirited and wanting to give up. The instructor controls the degree of stress during each lesson by increasing or decreasing his demands and expectations, sensitively adjusting them to the student's physical condition and emotional state.

Abiding patience is another trait that cannot be overstressed. Mobility skills take time to mature. Quick results cannot and should not be expected, by neither student nor instructor. Unsound practices, such as unrelenting pressure to perform well, a hurried instructional pace and unrealistic expectations are bound to boomerang.

When working with an adult, the instructor is less authoritative. He allows the student more room for self-direction than when working with a youngster, encouraging him to participate actively in planning objectives and to accept responsibility for his own progress.

The wise instructor nurtures a positive attitude, one that says: "I can do it; I won't give up." He is supportive at every turn, in the words he chooses, the gestures he makes, and with his facial expressions. Never threatening, he finds ways to bolster the student's sense of self-esteem, even when the student falls short of reaching a specific objective.

The instructor focuses on what the student can do, not on what he is unable to accomplish. His confidence spills over to the student and spurs him to explore his untapped resources. The instructor projects his conviction that the student can achieve reasonable objectives, even when the student feels hopeless about them. This unfailing support sustains the student when the going gets rough, calms his anxieties and fears, and fires his enthusiasm. It often means the difference between quitting or forging ahead, and it helps create a nurturing bond between instructor and student.

Usually the instructor has not personally experienced the disabling condition of his students. For this reason alone, the creative instructor continually searches for ways to learn from his students, rather than adhering rigidly to his role as an authority with all the answers. An open-minded approach adds to the instructor's fund of knowledge and understanding, and conveys a rightful recognition of the student's vital contribution to their joint endeavor.

The student clearly has a great deal to gain by taking training seriously and by cooperating with the instructor. It is to his advantage to make the most of an opportunity for growth which is not available to every disabled person. When possible, the student takes the initiative, openly discussing with the instructor any particular problems that might arise. Frank discussions can take place only within the security of a trusting relationship.

BEGIN TRAINING EARLY

For those born with a disability and those who become disabled during their early years, mobility training should begin as early as possible, in small, measured steps, carefully tailored to the child's physical and emotional readiness. The sooner the child gets on the right track with a positive attitude and the acquisition of basic skills, the better his chance of participating in life's activities and of growing into a self-reliant adult.

As straightforward as this may sound, it sometimes flies in the face of a natural tendency by parents to delay age-appropriate independence. This may be caused by their confusion about what they should expect from their child. A parent may feel that it is better to be safe than sorry, and consequently hold their child back from normal development. Overprotection may gain the upper hand over a more rational approach.

The child's readiness to travel cannot be gauged separately from his parents' readiness to encourage—or at least permit—such a forward step. Some parents require peer support or counseling to overcome their unwillingness to accept the inevitable risks associated with independent travel.

If a youngster hears too many safety rules all at once, confusion may result. A partially sighted 5-year-old girl, after being thoroughly briefed by her parents about crossing streets safely, summed up the main idea this way: "If you don't look both ways when you cross the street, you'll get hit by a red light!"

It is a mistake to assume that anyone who becomes disabled later in life should begin mobility training immediately after the onset of a disability. A recently-disabled person needs time to adjust to major transformations in his life, changes that may have occurred traumatically.

After the initial shock has worn off—a matter of days, weeks, or months—the patient should be assessed by a qualified specialist regarding the best timetable for mobility training. Ideally, this assessment would pool input from an array of professional workers: physician, nurse, physical therapist, occupational therapist, social worker, and psychologist. Their combined opinions offer the most reliable guidelines for individualized mobility training, and set the tone for a coordinated team approach, which is so vital to the patient's ultimate progress. It should not be overlooked that the patient himself is an important member of the team and gradually assumes greater responsibility for his own rehabilitation.

Some mobility assessments miss the mark by failing to take into account the desire, drive, and determination residing in the patient's heart. No judgement is complete that rests solely on a textbook interpretation of bodily dysfunction. The expectations that professionals communicate, both verbally or nonverbally, influence what goals the patient will attempt and accomplish. But the student himself ultimately determines how mobile he will become.

Following an initial adjustment period, the sooner the student begins mobility training, the better will be his chance for avoiding the harmful effects of languishing without hope or direction. Immersion in mobility training has the potential to boost the student's spirit, just as advances in other aspects of rehabilitation release energy that can be channeled into the development of mobility skills. There tends to be a reciprocal relationship between progress in mobility and advances in the student's overall rehabilitation. One influences the other in a continuous, healthy manner.

PRESENT LEVEL OF FUNCTIONING

A student with a deteriorating disability poses a puzzling problem for an instructor. Should lessons focus on the more severe disability looming in the future or on the student's present level of functioning?

A partially sighted woman, to use one example, is diagnosed as having an unstable eye condition that will eventually lead to total blindness.

Should the instructor require her to wear a blindfold during mobility lessons in preparation for travel as a totally blind person?

As a general rule, training should be geared to this woman's current degree of vision. Experience with a blindfold may be shattering to someone who cringes at the prospect of total blindness. Regardless of the prognosis, some people cling desparately, unrealistically to the hope that their vision will improve rather than worsen. Hope should not be yanked away from anyone before that person is emotionally ready to accept an unpalatable reality. The blindfold as a training tool should be used with discretion, and never forced on an unwilling student.

There are bound to be exceptions to this rule, as there are with any generalization about human beings. This woman might welcome, even request a blindfold during training as a practical way of preparing for eventual blindness. Although such reactions occur, they are more the exception than the rule.

The main point is that this question should be handled sensitively, with due consideration for the student's feelings. Adhering rigidly to one fixed policy—blindfold every partially sighted student, or permit no one to be blindfolded—would be counterproductive. Rigidity in any form violates a fundamental tenet of special education and rehabilitation. Every individual is unique and must be treated accordingly.

GRADUAL PROGRESSION OF TRAINING STEPS

Training should be organized in an orderly sequence consisting of a series of small steps, each step building on the preceding one in a gradual progression. Each step should be small enough to be mastered after no more than a few lessons, and represent a specific objective that makes enough sense to sustain the student's interest and motivation. Taking one small step at a time imposes less stress on the student than tackling large goals all at once. This also eases the strain on family members who are concerned about the student's progress.

The purpose of each step should be explained within the context of the overall mobility program, so the student comprehends how each lesson is logically connected with long-range goals. After the completion of each step, a minor celebration is in order, even if it's just a pat on the back, to raise the student's spirits as he faces the next step. Positive reinforcement adds a little fun to mobility training and serves as protection against setbacks, which are an ever-present possibility.

The student usually does not progress in a steady, forward direction. Relapses may occur at any time. The student may regress when training terminates because he misses encouragement from his instructor, or when he fails to find opportunities to travel.

Parts of one step may overlap with parts of subsequent lessons. The first objective, for example, might be to walk down a long corridor. The second objective, ascending stairs to the next floor, should include walking down the corridor to get to the stairway. Piggybacking one training step with a previous objective reinforces the earlier step and eases the transition from one training objective to the next.

The instructor regulates the pace of training by adjusting the frequency of lessons, such as twice a week, or once a month. He also controls the intensity of concentrated work. His professional judgment is based on continuous observation of the student's progress and relapses. Proceeding too slowly dulls the student's interest, but barreling ahead begs for a setback. As the instructor begins working with a young student, for example, he may decide that twenty minute sessions, which include casual conversation, might be the best way to start. Mobility is based on a diverse set of skills that cannot be acquired all at once. It calls for persistent effort over a considerable period.

Another reason for progressing gradually is to keep the lid on stress. The physical and mental rigors of independent travel may drain the student's inner resources. Each new step may arouse fresh waves of anxiety and require renewed determination. The student can best handle travel-related stress when challenges are parceled into bite-sized pieces.

Elderly mobility students cannot endure stress and pressure for long periods, so the instructor should shorten lessons and scatter brief rest periods throughout the lessons. Long routes, excessive work on stairs, and undue exposure to cold and wind should be avoided.

It is difficult for a nondisabled observer to appreciate the range of demands imposed by independent travel merely by watching someone in a wheelchair or a blind person travel. But insight can be gained by participating in role-playing exercises. Under reliable supervision, an interested party could walk blindfolded through a route, or try crossing a street while seated in a wheelchair. These experiences are "eye-openers." They sharpen awareness of the effort and patience required of both student and instructor, and provide a good opportunity for understanding the dynamics of mobility training.

Role-playing is a crucial component of educating mobility instructors who will work with people who are visually impaired. The soon-to-be instructors wear blindfolds as they travel with a cane throughout a city. This simulation of blindness is one of their most indispensible training experiences.

ONE-TO-ONE TEACHING RELATIONSHIP

Mobility training is best conducted on a one-to-one basis, one instructor working with one student. At the same time, appropriate support from special education or rehabilitation team members and from the student's family helps strengthen the learning process. Their contributions reinforce what the student has accomplished under the direct supervision of the mobility instructor.

Not only is a one-to-one relationship the best way for students to develop travel skills, it's also the most reliable means of assuring their personal safety during all stages of training. A one-to-one arrangement enables the instructor to control the element of risk by being keenly aware of his student's strengths and weaknesses, and by planning an individualized program based on that assessment.

The instructor must decide at what point in training his student is ready to travel independently, a decision that represents one of the most crucial turning points in mobility training. Only in a one-to-one relation-ship can the instructor make this decision responsibly, based on thorough knowledge of his student's abilities as demonstrated in previous lessons. Each student deserves the instructor's undivided attention, especially at hazardous spots such as street crossings.

A one-to-one teaching relationship affords the best opportunity to foster self-confidence and self-reliance. This principle is especially relevant when working with severely and multiply disabled students, who may require close, personal attention over an extended period to ensure progress. It is also the best way for the student and instructor to know and trust each other.

There are exceptions to the principle of individualized instruction. Complementary information, such as learning what travel-related words mean, could be taught to groups of two or more students closely matched in terms of mental development and mobility skills. A group of four retarded adolescents, for example, who had never traveled on a city bus, might benefit from a class on the use of fare boxes and transfers. They could also learn together how to read maps. A group of blind teenagers who travel separately into the city during mobility lessons might help each other by discussing their feelings about strangers who offer unsolicited assistance. A group of wheelchair users might exchange information about how to plan a problem-free trip. In general, group work is best reserved for discussions related to mobility, rather than for actually traveling through routes.

One of the main advantages of group instruction or group discussion is that more advanced students can serve as role models for those with less experience. Another advantage stems from the general pooling of each member's knowledge and experience.

Group instruction is also a practical way to stretch the use of the instructor's time, especially when qualified instructors are in short supply. But group instruction is best offered as an adjunct to individual training, not as a substitute for it. Working with groups is most effective when combined with individual lessons in real travel situations.

While working as a psychologist in Trondheim, Norway, I organized a mobility course for a group of eleven adults in wheelchairs. The chief aim of the course was to help the students become more willing travelers and to participate more often in social activities. I hoped that group discussions would enable the students to identify mobility obstacles, to figure out ways of circumventing them, to realize that all physically disabled travelers have mobility problems, and that the responsibility for eliminating mobility problems on the psychological plane rested with themselves.

Asking strangers for assistance was the first subject discussed. One student confided that it had taken him more than a year to conquer this particular problem. This discussion led to a role-playing situation where a student requested assistance from a nondisabled person. Talking afterwards about the role-playing, it was pointed out that the disabled person retains responsibility for specifying what help he needs, and for instructing an inexperienced helper about how that assistance should be rendered.

The students confided that it was easier to overcome discomfort about going somewhere for the first time when accompanied by another person, disabled or not. They observed that the most difficult part of going anywhere was making up one's mind to do so, and that advance planning prevented most mishaps and unwelcomed surprises.

It was agreed that each student should attempt going somewhere in his community where he had never been before, such as a restaurant or a movie, and then describe the outing at the next class session. One student with multiple sclerosis reported that she had gone shopping for the first time since becoming disabled. She had ordered transportation from the paratransit service, and had arranged beforehand to meet her sister-in-law in the store. The light yellow sweater she wore served as a fitting symbol of her proud achievement.

Another student reported that he had eaten in a restaurant in his office building for the first time in the year he had worked there. He viewed eating there as a challenge and was happy to report that he had the courage to go through with it.

The group listed problems that hinder mobility and then searched for ways to overcome each problem, such as lack of initiative, shyness, and worrying about the reactions of bystanders. They agreed that the hardest thing about travel was to make up one's mind to go somewhere.

While evaluating the course, several students suggested that a few nondisabled people should be invited to future mobility courses, so their views about contact with disabled people could be voiced. In the presence of disabled people, did they feel pity, guilt, fear or some other emotion? It was recommended that one class session should be conducted in a restaurant and that future mobility classes should be composed of an even balance of experienced travelers and novices. They hoped that future courses would offer mobility counseling between class sessions to individuals who requested it. The students liked the length of the course, which consisted of 6 sessions of about two and a half hours each, spaced two weeks apart.

The final class session took place during a weekend arranged at a hotel especially designed to meet the needs of guests with physical disabilities. One of the social highlights was wheelchair dancing. Everyone enjoyed moving to the music and I remember the pleasant experience of twirling my smiling partners in wheelchairs around the dance floor.

TRAINING IN THE STUDENT'S HOME NEIGHBORHOOD

No matter where training occurs, near a school or rehabilitation center, some lessons should take place in the student's home neighborhood. It cannot be assumed that skills acquired elsewhere will automatically be transferred to the home area which, after all, is where the student functions in everyday life. Some students make this adjustment on their own, but others require additional training to adapt skills learned in other locations to their home neighborhood. These lessons also make it easier for family members to observe training, to participate more actively in the training process, and to support the efforts of both the student and instructor.

Traveling at night differs in many respects from daytime travel, so evening practice sessions should be arranged when possible, especially for those who anticipate traveling at night, but feel afraid to do so.

FOLLOW-UP TRAINING

After the completion of mobility training, it is useful to check periodically on the student's progress. Follow-up lessons are especially useful when a student changes neighborhoods, begins working at a new worksite, or when the instructor senses that the student will regress after training terminates. A request for follow-up lessons might be initiated by the student's vocational counselor, by a family member, or by the student himself.

Follow-up training focuses on specific problems. Usually limited to one or two lessons, it is a means of spot-checking on the student's progress. When a retarded student, for example, graduates from high school and must learn a new route from his home to a workshop, a few follow-up lessons would be helpful.

For school-age students, the follow-up phase of training may occur periodically over the course of years. Some students receive training sporadically during elementary school, additional work in middle school and advanced lessons in high school on public transportation. Some receive training only during their last year of school. The pattern of mobility training within each school system is determined by student needs, administrative policy and the availability of mobility instructors.

CHAPTER 6

DEPENDENT VS. INDEPENDENT MOBILITY

The primary aim of mobility instruction is to enable people with disabilities to travel as independently as possible, without relying unnecessarily on others. Many disabled people, however, cannot reach a level of mobility even remotely resembling independence. For them, dependence is an unavoidable and pervasive fact of everyday life.

A negative connotation is often attached to the term dependent mobility. At best, it is viewed as a temporary phase to be passed through quickly—a necessary detour on the road to independence. At worst, it labels a permanent condition associated with a severely restricted lifestyle.

Dependent mobility conjures up images of hopelessness and helplessness, of failure to benefit from training, of insufficient willpower, of a depressing, dehumanizing way of life. These negative images erect barriers between service providers and those who require assistance in getting about, further adding to their isolation and immobility. An instructor may feel like a failure if his student remains dependent, despite the instructor's best efforts.

People close to the disabled person sometimes foster dependency and discourage any striving toward independence. This might be due to a misguided attempt to eliminate the risk of injury or a preference for relating with the disabled person in that way. Another possibility is that the disabled person may choose, for personal reasons, to remain dependent and isolated. But in time, the disabled person may become weary of a dependent lifestyle, and seek mobility training or counseling to strengthen his self-help skills.

Incidental learning occurs even while a disabled person takes a trip with another person who leads the way. Passive mobility, making a trip while dependent on another person, is preferable to being shut-in without any chance for getting outside. It is also a means of preparing for eventual trips alone. A child who accompanies his parents to a shopping mall, for example, learns a good deal about shopping and about how to get there, even though he is completely dependent on his parents for safety and direction.

For these reasons, it is a good idea to include disabled children in family outings as a way of enlarging their experience and preparing them for independence. In a similar way, field trips arranged during the school day generate important contact with the outside world for disabled students. The same idea holds true for disabled adults who cannot get around on their own. They should be included in shopping trips and family outings whenever possible.

Dependent and independent mobility appear to be distinct categories, but in practice, both coexist, blending together in shifting proportions. Some people travel unaided indoors, but depend on others for travel outdoors. Some are independent while traveling outdoors, but seek assistance at busy street crossings.

No one is completely independent. But some people go through a superindependent stage when they will accept absolutely no help from anyone, clinging to the illusion that they are totally self-reliant. We all have pockets of dependency. We all rely on others for certain kinds of help: On bus drivers, auto mechanics, travel agents, or on a gas station attendant for directions.

A self-reliant wheelchair user looks for assistance when he reaches an uncut curb or when snow blocks his path. How many of us seek the company of a friend to go to an event when we would feel uncomfortable going alone? All of us need to find an acceptable balance between doing things on our own and relying on others. A well-adjusted adult acknowledges the fact that human beings are interdependent.

The ultimate goal of training is not total, uncompromising independence. Rather, it is the cultivation of a sensible, realistic attitude based on a healthy acceptance of one's limitations and on the practical necessity of relying on others for appropriate help.

It is possible to preserve an inner sense of dignity, even while being led by a guide or pushed in a wheelchair. A human being can exude a proud, self-respecting spirit even while accepting help. It is essentially a matter of embracing a positive attitude. An experienced blind traveler readily accepts help crossing a street even though he is capable of crossing alone. Accepting help makes the crossing easier, without threatening his ego or competence. It also eliminates one extra strain from the day's chores.

There is ample room for individual initiative and resourcefulness even while accepting help. The person in a wheelchair who requires assistance getting up a few steps still retains the responsibility for figuring out how to secure assistance. When help arrives, he still bears the responsibility for instructing his helpers in an amiable manner about the right way of assisting, so that neither the person in the wheelchair nor the helpers suffers an injury.

Even though a blind jogger stays close to his sighted running companion, he is asserting himself in a positive way. He may be providing an incentive for his companion, who enjoys the results of exercise, but is lackadaisical about getting started. The blind person initiated the run and arranged for the companion to meet him at a certain place at a specific time.

The act of securing assistance may be viewed in a positive light, as a challenge to the traveler's ingenuity. The overriding concern is that the traveler decide where he wants to go and that he remains determined to get there. How he gets there is of secondary importance. A disabled person may require help to go to a meeting, but his contribution to the assembled group is no less valued because of the help he received in getting there.

When inquiring about directions, the disabled traveler must ask questions in an intelligible manner to elicit the information he wants. In that sense, asking for directions is not a passive act. As the student realizes that prudent use of assistance does not threaten his integrity or independence, the need to prove himself to other people diminishes.

A severely disabled individual, who requires considerable assistance to manage a trip, would be well-advised to avoid planning an excursion that hinges heavily on help from strangers. While many Good Samaritans are ready to assist, some people do not want to take the time or trouble to help those who need it. The most essential help should be arranged for in advance, not left to chance. Hiring an attendant or driver may spell the difference between traveling outside one's home or being homebound, even if this arrangement is only temporary. During an illness or pregnancy, a disabled person may decide to take cabs more often than usual.

The disabled traveler may have fewer choices in the total range of travel options, so the accessible ones must be used to maximum advantage. Part of the responsibility of those who teach mobility is to increase the traveler's awareness of all travel options and to encourage an informed choice, without making moral judgments about personal mobility habits. The travel needs of some disabled people may be best served by finding someone willing to accompany them for assistance and companionship.

Chapter 7

PSYCHOLOGICAL AND SOCIAL BARRIERS

It is a short-sighted mistake to imagine that structural barriers—steps, narrow passageways, inaccessible lavatories—are the only, or even the primary cause of travel impediments. Although architectural barriers pose the most obvious roadblocks, they represent only one aspect of the problem, one side of the mobility coin.

On the opposite side of that coin are social and psychological barriers, vague feelings of uneasiness and apprehension, diffuse anxieties and habitual worries, specific fears and paralyzing phobias. These psychological problems can affect all aspects of mobility and squelch a person's natural striving toward freedom of movement. Unless emotional hindrances are recognized as a fundamental cause of travel difficulties, effective remedial action is obstructed.

Fears often stem from social contacts. They grow out of the necessity of interacting with the public, virtual strangers, who are not always sensitive to the needs and feelings of people with disabilities. Well-meaning bystanders may be annoyingly oversolicitous, insisting on giving more help than is wanted. Others may callously ignore a disabled person, even when his need for assistance is obvious. Still others grow impatient if their waiting line is momentarily delayed by a disabled person.

Emotional barriers are more crippling than any bodily or mental impairment for some travelers, but remain a minor concern for others. Fear may be a dominant factor only in the early phases of learning to travel, or it may persist throughout the course of mobility training. Some degree of anxiety is natural and can be expected. A moderate amount may even enhance the learning process by keeping the traveler alert. But any serious search for the underlying causes of travel problems must include attention to the traveler's internal blocks.

The degree to which psychological barriers restrict mobility varies with such factors as the traveler's personality, the degree to which he has adjusted to his disability, and the general circumstances of his life. The person who has adjusted well to his disability is probably more fettered by architectural barriers than by emotional ones. For the person who has not progressed that far, accessibility remains secondary to his tendency of avoiding travel for emotional reasons. It is easier to talk about inaccessible buildings than to face one's inner fears.

Fears are most debilitating during the early stages of adjustment, when travel demands may appear to be so overwhelming that the disabled person refuses to leave his residence. Some fears are appropriate and rational, generating a heightened readiness to cope with real difficulties. Some worries and fears simply evaporate with experience and maturity. Other emotional barriers require timely support from family or peers. The most deep-seated fears and phobias call for professional counseling.

The important point is that mobility problems stem from both physical and psychological causes. Any attempt to resolve travel problems by concentrating solely on physical causes or solely on psychological causes is bound to miss the mark.

Fear is one of the most common psychological barrier and the one that interferes most often with mobility. It is the enemy of mobility. The milder form is called anxiety, a vague, uneasy feeling without a specific cause, referred to colloquially as "having butterflies." Fear in its most compulsive form escalates into a phobia, a severe physiological and mental response that can cause panic reactions and paralyze physical movement. Some fears are universal. All of us suffer from them to some degree at one time or another—such as dread of physical injury and apprehension about seeking assistance from strangers.

The alert instructor recognizes the pressure that fears exert on his student. He scrutinizes those fears and devises strategies to help his student cope with their origins and consequences. In an attempt to desensitize his student, the instructor encourages him to verbalize fearful feelings.

In the following section, some of the most prevalent fears associated with mobility are identified and described, along with suggestions for allaying their negative influence. Separately or in combination, fears constitute a formidable mobility barrier that must be reduced or eliminated before true freedom of movement can be achieved.

FEAR OF THE UNKNOWN

Fear of the unknown, one of the most common fears, stems from a lack of confidence when traveling in unfamiliar areas. Faced with the prospect of traveling on a new route or entering a new building, a flood of unanswered questions assault the traveler's mind: Will the route be too complicated? Will the corridor be too crowded? Will there be too many stairs? Will assistance be available? Can I handle unexpected problems that might arise?

As the grip of this fear tightens, it chokes off the impulse to go to new places and to join in normal social activities. This apprehension narrows the person's range of experience, squeezing a full life into a few comfortable routines. Uncertainty about coping with new travel problems may become so threatening that it outweighs the enticement of new experiences.

The power of fear to interfere with mobility depends on the traveler's resolve to confront his fearful feelings. Left unchecked, fear erodes the person's motivation to broaden his horizons, imposing a restricted pattern of living that becomes increasingly difficult to alter.

Donald, a 19-year-old paraplegic in a wheelchair, is leery of going to new places. A friend invites him to a lecture on photography in a public auditorium he had never before entered. Even though the lecture interests Donald, photography being his hobby, he is uncertain about how to manage a long flight of stairs leading up to the front entrance. He is insecure about navigating through milling crowds without colliding with someone.

Afraid to take real or imagined risks and reluctant to seek information, he politely declines the invitation, choosing to remain in the safe surroundings of his apartment. Donald rationalizes his decision by remembering that his favorite TV program is scheduled for that evening.

This decision reinforces Donald's fear of the unknown. When the next opportunity arises to test himself in unfamiliar surroundings, his resistance may have stiffened, leaving Donald fortified behind an isolating wall of self-protection.

The only way to break this vicious cycle is by taking assertive steps to loosen the grip of this fear. Donald could be encouraged to gather information beforehand about the number and location of the stairs, and ways to circumvent them, and about other details that preyed on his mind. Armed with relevant facts, he could devise a rational plan that would whittle his fears down to a manageable size. Constructive suggestions and emotional support from a mobility instructor or other helper would aid Donald win his battle against fear.

Donald could also visit the building sometime before the lecture, as a kind of rehearsal, to acquaint himself with its special features. If he scouted the place at an uncrowded time, he would feel less conspicuous and hurried. A frank talk about his mobility concerns with the friend who had invited him might also help. Perhaps the friend could join him on a familiarization trip, turning it into a pleasant social outing rather than a dreaded chore.

When Estelle, a blind woman in New York City, began mobility training, she was nervous about going anywhere alone. Her instructor, recognizing her fragile nerves, guided Estelle through unfamiliar buildings and new routes, leisurely describing the surroundings and notable landmarks. During that early period, he never suggested that she travel unescorted. These casual excursions, with her instructor at her side, calmed her nerves to the point that she could eventually travel alone, even on unfamiliar routes.

Fear of the unknown might be especially strong in a retarded youngster who hasn't yet learned to recognize and trust his own capabilities. A few familiarization trips would be helpful before expecting him to travel alone, the number of trips depending on his travel abilities and degree of impairment.

FEAR OF SEEKING ASSISTANCE FROM STRANGERS

Fear may prevent a traveler from approaching strangers, even with a legitimate reason for seeking assistance or information. This problem may be linked with resentment of his dependency or an unwillingness to admit his need for assistance. It may also be caused by an unwillingness to feel obligated, or by apprehension about contact with potentially dangerous strangers. With time, experience, and guidance, the student realizes that seeking assistance in an appropriate way, even in the seemingly cold indifference of a large city, is a normal part of a healthy adjustment for anyone who travels.

Let's return to Donald, the young man in a wheelchair, who finds that the only way to ascend three steps in front of a building is by asking strangers to lift him in his wheelchair. If he shies away from making this request, due to fear, embarrassment or false pride, he will have to abandon his goal of getting up those steps and into the building. But Donald may decide that the best solution is to wait until some of his friends are available to assist, because they know his needs. He cringes at the thought of approaching total strangers, who may resent this imposition or even turn their backs on him.

The real barrier is not the stairs. It's Donald's emotional conflict about asking someone for help. Getting up the stairs is a physical problem. The dread of seeking assistance is a psychological one.

Everett, a partially sighted man, rejects the idea of using a white cane because he recoils at the thought of being identified as a blind man. He learned by experience how to pass as a fully sighted person, concealing from everyone any clues about his secret impairment. One consequence of this pretense is that he refuses to ask such simple questions as, "What number is on that bus?" He would rather walk several blocks out of his way than "humiliate" himself by exposing his visual limitations.

For Everett, this detour is worth the inconvenience because it enables him to keep intact an image of himself as a fully sighted person, an image that has become a major part of his psychological make-up. He also fears that people will not readily believe that he is visually impaired. They might even become suspicious when an apparently nondisabled person asks such an obvious question as, "What number is on that bus?" It is easier for bystanders to respond appropriately when they recognize a person with an obvious disability, such as total blindness.

There is a healthy side to this assertion of pride and determination, the side that says: "I will not let my disability stand in my way." Everett went through school with sighted students. None of his friends had visual problems, so he learned how to fit into their way of living and his self-identity became that of a sighted person.

A hearing impaired traveler, afraid of being misunderstood or ridiculed because of his conspicuous manner of communicating, may avoid asking anyone for information, regardless of the inconvenience caused by this avoidance. He has a nagging uneasiness about facing emergencies: Whom would he turn to for help in a difficult situation, and how would he communicate his needs? In time, he may accept the need to write down his questions when gestures fail to convey his meaning, and to become more open about his special needs.

An avoidance response could be curbed by encouraging the student to initiate ordinary conversation with new acquaintances. Or the student could approach salespersons, or even begin with conversations on the telephone, if that's less threatening than face-to-face contact. Small, insignificant requests can be gradually injected into the conversation, such as asking for the correct time, or the day's date or the location of the nearest telephone. As confidence grows, the requests reflect more closely the student's real needs.

With experience, the student gains a realistic sense of what kinds of assistance can be reasonably expected from strangers, what manner of approach should be used and what tone of voice best expresses his sincere desire to be helped. He gains an appreciation of the value of these skills in relation to his overall travel competencies.

Role-playing exercises heighten awareness of human dynamics in social situations. The student asks a "salesclerk" (enacted by someone else) where to find household appliances in an imaginary department store. Once both actors understand their roles and can visualize the situation, their dialogue is improvised. After each role-playing session, the student benefits from the observers' comments: Did he make eye contact with the clerk, or did a blind student aim his voice in the direction of the clerk? The person playing the role of the clerk could frankly explain how he felt during the exchange, thus offering the student a glimpse into how his words and manner are perceived by others.

Some elderly people refrain from contacting strangers because they feel vulnerable, more at risk of being taken advantage of. Some don't want to admit that their physical powers have diminished to the point that they require help. A lifetime of pride in being independent may stand in the way. Such people would rather stay at home than request assistance. They don't want to risk being embarrassed in awkward situations, or being mugged by attackers who prey on the elderly.

A disabled person may have experienced the disappointment of receiving misinformation from a stranger, a set of directions that led to hopeless confusion. During mobility lessons, the instructor helps the student to select a passerby who appears likely to answer responsibly, rather than turning to the first person who happens to come along.

FEAR OF BEING STARED AT

Some travelers avoid casual trips because they fear that other people will stare at them. Most people dislike attention from strangers. This discourtesy creates uncomfortable psychological pressure and increases the emotional cost of traveling. Even when the actual demands of the trip fall within range of the traveler's competencies, his impulse to travel may be stifled by anticipation of stares that reflect pity, prying curiosity, or outright rejection.

Despite efforts to remain inconspicuous, he feels that the public persistently invades his privacy, compounding a gnawing sense of alienation. When entering a store, he expects concerned clerks and puzzled patrons to watch his every move. He may avoid restaurants for fear of dropping food on the floor and having people fix stares of reprimand on his clumsiness. Even though blind people cannot see other people's stares, they quickly sense extraordinary attention directed at them.

Social isolation is one of the most serious problems faced by deaf and hearing impaired people. A deaf teenager named Myra has no difficulty traveling from her home to a downtown shopping center, but she avoids that trip because she is sensitive about the stares she attracts while communicating with sign language or when writing notes. It bothers her to draw attention to her deafness. Even though her self-consciousness evaporates in the company of deaf people, she remains mobility-limited when traveling alone. Part of the difficulty stems from the fact that Myra is a sensitive adolescent. If she doesn't become less sensitive as time passes, counseling may help her to overcome this problem.

The natural curiosity of children causes them to stare wide-eyed at anyone out of the ordinary. A mother noticed her young child staring at a man in a wheelchair. She eased this awkward situation by saying, "Please excuse my son, but he's never seen such a big stroller before!" In other cases, however, mothers rush their child away saying, "Don't look," when a few calm words of explanation would have sufficed.

Strangers sometimes offer disabled people money or other gifts as tokens of their feelings of pity or guilt, or simply as an expression of their goodwill. Unsolicited gifts, however, add a concrete dimension to the problem of being stared at, of attracting unwanted attention. It is one more indication that disabled travelers are often denied privacy and anonymity.

Donald, seated in his wheelchair, cashed a check in a shopping center and was in the process of putting the bills into a small leather bag on his lap. A passing woman, noticing the bag containing money, stopped and slipped some change into his bag. Donald called her back immediately and returned her unsolicited donation. He told her in a polite but firm way that he could not accept her gift and thanked her anyway. He took pride in setting a good example. It was important for him to do his share of public education. He enjoyed making other people aware of the dignity and capabilities of disabled people. He delighted in transforming the stares of strangers into opportunities for meaningful contact.

No one wants to relinquish his or her sense of privacy or personal space, even while wading through crowds. This basic human right is no less valued by people with disabilities, who may be even more sensitive to indiscretions that make them feel different from others.

During my training as a mobility instructor, I walked blindfolded with a cane on miles of Boston sidewalks, experiencing first-hand how bystanders react to a sightless person. They assumed I was blind and I could sense from their tense silence that many pairs of eyes were tracking my every move. Walking just a few steps beyond them, still within earshot, I heard whispered but audible sentiments such as, "Isn't it a shame?" or "What a pity!" They seemed to think that, since I was blind, I could not hear them. Their hushed exchanges almost distracted me at a time when full concentration was required. Out of necessity, I ignored their comments and attended to the task of navigating safely.

A disabled person's companion or helper might perceive the extra attention as being directed toward him, rather than the disabled person. As a result, the companion or helper may hesitate to be seen in public with a disabled person, further complicating the disabled person's problems. In such a bind, the disabled person would do well to reassure his companion and help him shed reluctance or self-consciousness about being seen in public with a disabled person.

FEAR OF PHYSICAL DANGER

This fear stems from misgivings about real dangers along the traveler's path. Although this fear affects everyone to some degree, it is especially troublesome for a disabled traveler, who is more vulnerable to indoor and outdoor hazards than people who can evade them more easily.

Fear of physical danger breeds the notion that it is wiser to remain in safe surroundings than risk venturing into an ominous world filled with countless pitfalls and lurking dangers. Someone who became disabled as the result of an accident or a criminal assault might feel particularly plagued by this apprehension.

Picture the blind woman, Estelle, walking across a street, swinging her cane in a sweeping motion. Her keenest fear may be of plunging into an open manhole, undetected by her cane, or of being struck by a speeding automobile. This fear is compounded when facing the prospect of going out alone at night.

Fear of physical danger has the power to undermine confidence and destroy the desire to travel. The success or failure of mobility training might hinge on how squarely this fear is confronted and brought under control. The instructor helps the student evaluate the reality of physical dangers through experiences during mobility lessons and discussions afterward.

The student gradually learns to distinguish between real and exaggerated dangers, between avoidable hazards and those that cannot be eliminated, but must be accepted as a normal part of travel. Some fears of hazards are temporary, such as being afraid of traveling on ice-covered sidewalks. The mobility student learns to use his common sense, to anticipate problems and to take reasonable precautions. He learns that being overly anxious leads to more problems than being relaxed. As fear diminishes, he feels less fatigued.

The instructor modifies his teaching strategy when working with a fearful student. Since Estelle is afraid of being injured while crossing a street and seems to freeze up just before crossing, the instructor selects routes which involve easy-to-cross streets, with no fast-moving traffic to bother his student. He stays close by, walking right alongside her while crossing, minimizing pressure in every way possible. To help her relax, his manner is casual, unhurried and reassuring, marked by friendly conversation. He makes the occasion more like a pleasant outing than a mobility lesson. The whole learning process is slowed down and made less intense, less threatening. The student remains alert to the dangers of street crossings, but feels less intimidated by them.

On the other hand, however, the problem is not too much fear but too little, especially among youngsters. They may have little if any sense of the dangers posed by crossings, so they are eager to charge into a street with a naive belief that drivers will watch out for them. The mobility instructor must continually point out potential dangers until the student fully realizes the hazards.

In large cities, major crimes against elderly people, including robbery, rape, and murder, have become an ugly fact of urban life. This violent campaign against elderly citizens has been linked to the mushrooming use of drugs among desperate young people whose grim hopes for the future have eaten away their social consciousness. Elderly people may feel especially vulnerable to being mugged or otherwise taken advantage of by neighborhood thugs because would-be assailants may view them as easy targets.

This fear channels many elderly people into restricted travel patterns. Some are leery about going anywhere during the day and never go out at night. The more anxious among them have resorted to keeping guns in their homes, to be used as a last resort in case of home invasion.

FEAR OF DISCOVERING ONE'S REAL LIMITATIONS

As long as a student's mobility competencies remain untested in real situations, it is easy for him to imagine that he actually has no travel limitations. Before coming to terms with his disability, he may be tempted to ignore the harsher realities of having a disability and cling to an overly optimistic view of his capabilities. A disabled person might shield his travel abilities from the test of experience for fear of discovering his actual weaknesses and limitations. He might delude himself into thinking that he could go to more places if he wanted to, but that he has no desire to enlarge his circle of activities. Such rationalizing leaves intact his underlying fear, dimming prospects for increasing his mobility.

An adolescent, in the throes of discovering his emerging identity, might be especially unwilling to acknowledge his real limitations. The person who becomes disabled as a teenager or adult may continue to believe he retains the same range of mobility he previously enjoyed. This form of denial, of clinging to unreal expectations, blocks the person from dealing with his limitations constructively. It may be linked to a deeply-felt hope that somehow the disability will disappear.

This attitude may be aggravated by parents and other family members who, because of their own needs, fan the fires of unrealistic hope for a miraculous recovery. Some parents, unable to accept their child's disability, look for relief by its disappearance. If they continue to delude themselves, it becomes more difficult for the child to accept his limits. Clinging to illusions or unfounded hopes interferes with practical strategies to build mobility skills and dilutes the motivation to use them. The disabled person is then more likely to stagnate, not only in mobility, but in his overall activities and personal development.

A realistic assessment of the student's capabilities and potential at the beginning of mobility training helps the student face the true dimensions of his travel problems. If necessary, the student should be referred to a counselor who would probe the roots of his unwillingness to deal with his altered circumstances.

Another possibility, which can never be discounted, is that the disabled person himself, in his own good time, will reach a point where he resolves to do everything in his power to push back the barriers that frustrate his natural urge for mobility. At that point, he will drop pretenses and self-deceptions and take stock of what he really can and cannot do. Some people reach this point on their own, and prefer to do so. Others require professional assistance, or at least moral support from family and friends.

FEAR OF BEING ALONE IN PUBLIC PLACES

A disabled person might be hesitant to venture into public places, not because of physical dangers or the need to ask for help, but due to fear of being alone in crowded or even vacant areas. This fear influences decisions about going anywhere, even for people who have no physical or mental impairment other than this apprehension.

This fear may snowball to such proportions that it must be classified as a phobia. The psychiatric term coined to identify this incapacitating reaction is **agoraphobia**, which literally means a fear of open places. There is no single cause for this condition and its origins are unknown. Agoraphobia usually surfaces in people who have no disability other than this petrifying fear.

People with agoraphobia are terrified about traveling anywhere alone, especially where there are crowds, such as in shopping areas. At the mere thought of venturing outside, they grow visibly agitated, break into a cold sweat, become dizzy, or hyperventilate. They may remain at home for months, sometimes years at a time without stepping outdoors, prisoners in their own homes, unable to go anywhere alone. They protect themselves in this way against what is perceived to be a terror-filled world.

In response to the potency and prevalence of agoraphobia, individual and group therapy programs have emerged internationally. Essentially, the client takes short trips accompanied by a therapist, mobility specialist, or helper, beginning with simple outings to uncrowded places. The therapist stays close to the client, dispensing emotional support every step of the way. If a client has a specific fear of riding an escalator, the therapist stands next to him on the escalator until his symptoms abate.

Gradually, the trips are extended to more crowded places. The therapist increases the distance between himself and the client until solo trips can be made comfortably, without signs of emotional distress, until the client loses his overwhelming impulse to flee. These therapeutic excursions help the patient understand what triggers his imaginary fears. He learns to monitor his fluctuating emotions and to gain control by shifting his attention from frightening preoccupations to reassuring elements in his environment.

A prominent figure in establishing therapeutic programs to combat agoraphobia is a New York psychiatrist, Manuel D. Zane. Dr. Zane's interest in this phobia grew out of his professional work with orthopedically impaired patients.

A related phenomenon is called **cocooning,** a lifestyle in which people with or without a disability become voluntarily homebound, their freedom of movement shut down by a perception of the world as being rife with imminent dangers. In contrast to agoraphobia, people leading this reclusive lifestyle function normally in certain respects, such as traveling to and from work. But aside from those exceptions, they choose to remain at home whenever possible.

FEAR OF GETTING LOST

Dread of getting lost, feeling hopeless about reaching a chosen destination—these feelings are shared by almost everyone at one time or another. But here again, fear of getting lost may be more keenly felt by a disabled traveler who feels less in control of his travel abilities, more threatened by the prospect of helplessness and the necessity of depending on the kindness of others.

This fear is closely allied to the fear of asking for help from strangers. Once progress has been made in a willingness to approach strangers with specific requests, there is less chance that fear of getting lost will spoil one's travel plans.

Some training exercises are specifically designed to teach the student how to deal with disorientation. When a student strays from a chosen route, the instructor stops the student and helps him to retrace his steps mentally, so the student can detect where he made the error that threw him off course. Or the instructor might walk with the student back to the point where he deviated from the planned course, physically retracing his steps.

In mobility training with visually impaired students, finding one's way back to a familiar point and of reorienting oneself, is called **recovery**. It is sometimes combined with another exercise called the **drop-off lesson**, in which the student agrees to be intentionally disoriented by being led a few blocks away from the route he has been learning. Then, relying on his own resources, the student finds his way back to the familiar path.

FEAR OF NOT FINDING A RESTROOM

This practical concern can scuttle travel plans just as surely as any deep-rooted anxiety. No trip can be casually envisioned without taking into account the location and accessibility of restrooms. Uncertainty about adequate toilet facilities can pour cold water on any travel plans.

For wheelchair users, it is not only a matter of locating the men's or ladies' room, but of making sure that the toilet portal is wide enough for the chair to pass through unimpeded, with ample turning space to manuever the wheelchair. When traveling with a helper, the wheelchair user must feel assured that, if a time-consuming detour becomes necessary to reach an accessible restroom, the helper would make the detour in a willing spirit.

Worries about restrooms can be whittled down by gleaning relevant information from access guides and from knowledgeable acquaintances. It is also helpful if the disabled person has a frank understanding with his companion, so assistance can be counted on, even if it involves inconvenient changes of plans. As soon as the traveler enters a building, he should find out the location of the restroom, before it becomes urgent to do so. When an experienced traveler knows that it will be difficult to locate a restroom in certain situations, he reduces his intake of liquids for a few hours beforehand.

The person who resists speaking to strangers is more vulnerable to this fear because questions about restrooms might seem especially embarrassing. As the fear of asking for help lessens, a corresponding reduction can be expected in the fear of not finding a restroom, setting the traveler free of a major worry.

All of the fears described in this chapter are by no means confined to people with disabilities. They affect most of us, to one degree or another, at one time or another, in one form or another, in one combination or another. They may be temporary problems that appear occasionally or only in the early stages of learning to travel.

Nevertheless, these fears should be recognized as an insidious force that creates bodily tension, mental anguish, and has the power to shackle travel ambitions. When motivation is strong enough to overcome avoidance tendencies, it is possible to combat unfounded fears. If fears are openly acknowledged and squarely confronted, they can be reduced to manageable proportions, and the traveler can free himself of these paralyzing emotions.

In time, the traveler realizes that fantasized dangers, though keenly felt, are harmless; that worries are more debilitating than real experiences. Having experienced the negative effects of irrational fears, the prudent traveler stays alert to circumstances that might cause him to push the panic button. It bears repeating that some disabled people wrestle with and conquer these fears on their own, but others may require a helping hand from professionals, family members, or friends, or some combination of these resources.

APPENDIX

Curriculum Model

The curriculum model in the following pages is based on a task analysis of some of the main challenges a person with a disability must confront while traveling. Each task is subdivided into smaller steps so that they can be more easily mastered by the student. The steps are organized in a learning hierarchy, or learning ladder, with simpler skills placed at the top of each page and more complex ones lower down. This is a graphic way to picture the process by which complex skills are built on simpler ones. This curriculum model is suggestive rather than exhaustive.

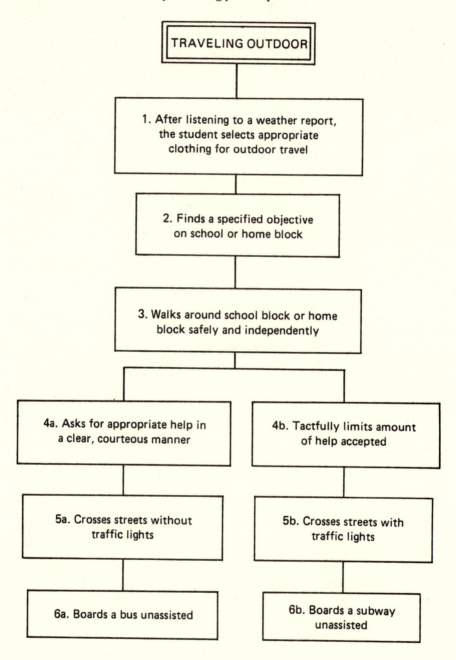

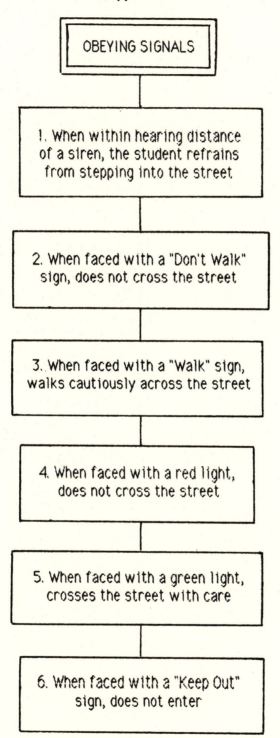

OBEYING SIGNALS

1. When within hearing distance of a siren, the student refrains from stepping into the street

2. When faced with a "Don't Walk" sign, does not cross the street

3. When faced with a "Walk" sign, walks cautiously across the street

4. When faced with a red light, does not cross the street

5. When faced with a green light, crosses the street with care

6. When faced with a "Keep Out" sign, does not enter

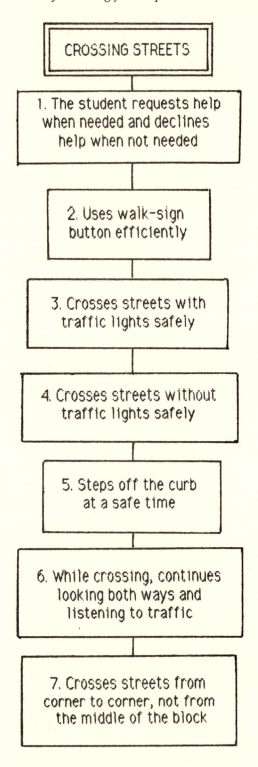

CROSSING STREETS

1. The student requests help when needed and declines help when not needed

2. Uses walk-sign button efficiently

3. Crosses streets with traffic lights safely

4. Crosses streets without traffic lights safely

5. Steps off the curb at a safe time

6. While crossing, continues looking both ways and listening to traffic

7. Crosses streets from corner to corner, not from the middle of the block

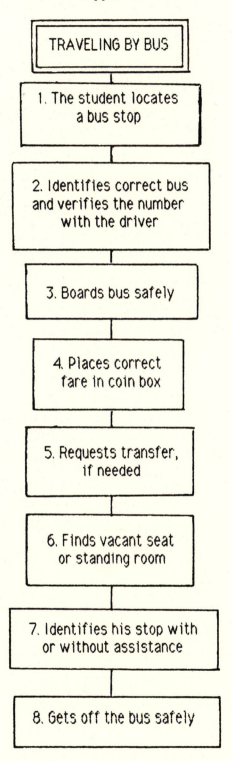

TRAVELING BY BUS

1. The student locates
a bus stop

2. Identifies correct bus
and verifies the number
with the driver

3. Boards bus safely

4. Places correct
fare in coin box

5. Requests transfer,
if needed

6. Finds vacant seat
or standing room

7. Identifies his stop with
or without assistance

8. Gets off the bus safely

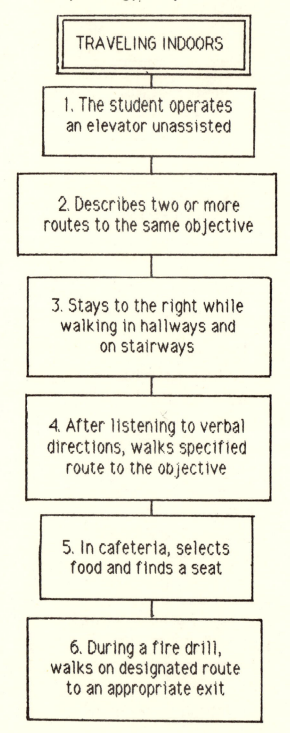

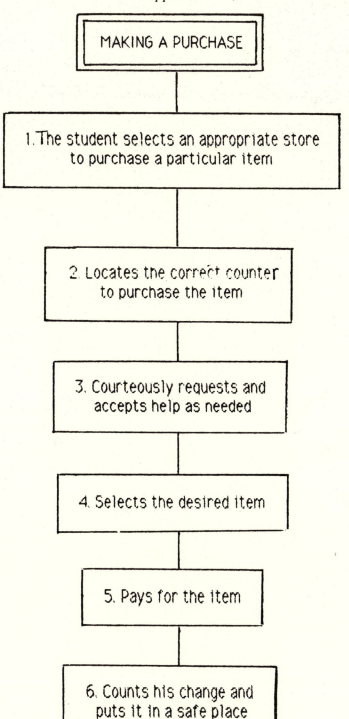

MAKING A PURCHASE

1. The student selects an appropriate store to purchase a particular item

2. Locates the correct counter to purchase the item

3. Courteously requests and accepts help as needed

4. Selects the desired item

5. Pays for the item

6. Counts his change and puts it in a safe place

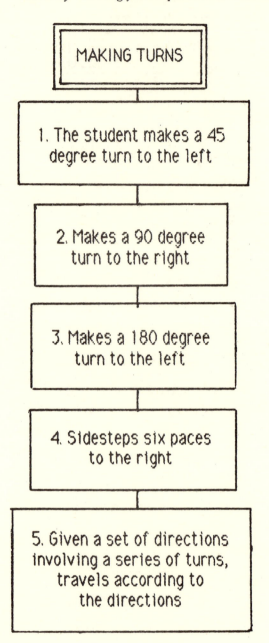

MAKING TURNS

1. The student makes a 45 degree turn to the left

2. Makes a 90 degree turn to the right

3. Makes a 180 degree turn to the left

4. Sidesteps six paces to the right

5. Given a set of directions involving a series of turns, travels according to the directions

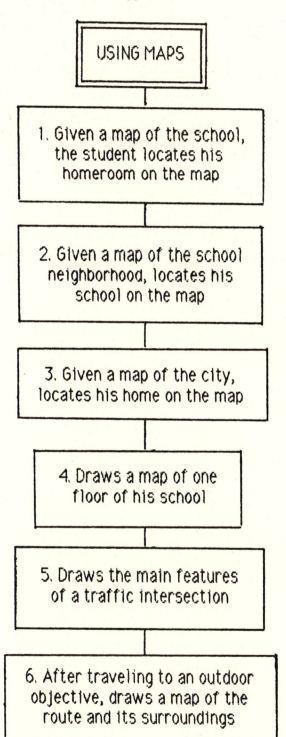

USING MAPS

1. Given a map of the school, the student locates his homeroom on the map

2. Given a map of the school neighborhood, locates his school on the map

3. Given a map of the city, locates his home on the map

4. Draws a map of one floor of his school

5. Draws the main features of a traffic intersection

6. After traveling to an outdoor objective, draws a map of the route and its surroundings

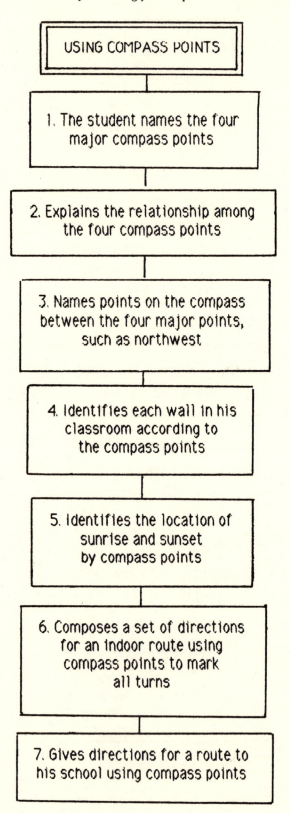

USING COMPASS POINTS

1. The student names the four major compass points

2. Explains the relationship among the four compass points

3. Names points on the compass between the four major points, such as northwest

4. Identifies each wall in his classroom according to the compass points

5. Identifies the location of sunrise and sunset by compass points

6. Composes a set of directions for an indoor route using compass points to mark all turns

7. Gives directions for a route to his school using compass points

ESTIMATING DISTANCES,
HEIGHTS AND TIME

1. In a classroom, the student estimates the
distance from one wall to the opposite wall

2. Estimates the distance across
a street, from corner to corner

3. Estimates the number of miles
from New York to San Francisco

4. Estimates the height of
his instructor

5. Estimates the height of
his classroom

6. Estimates the time required
to travel a specified outdoor route

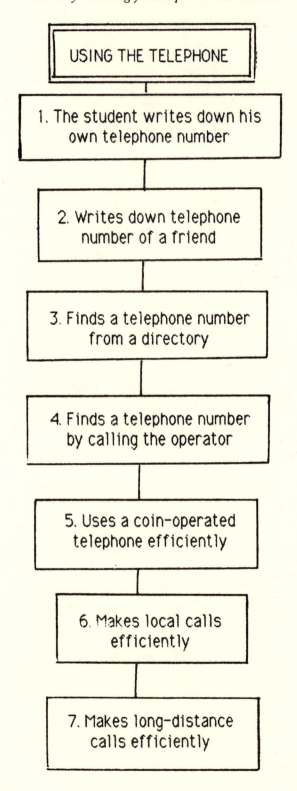

USING THE TELEPHONE

1. The student writes down his own telephone number

2. Writes down telephone number of a friend

3. Finds a telephone number from a directory

4. Finds a telephone number by calling the operator

5. Uses a coin-operated telephone efficiently

6. Makes local calls efficiently

7. Makes long-distance calls efficiently

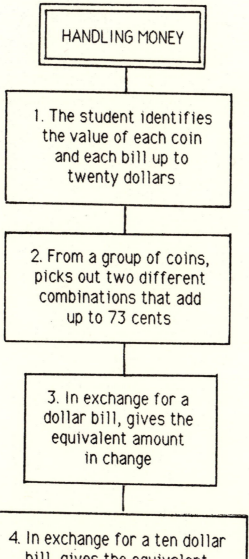

HANDLING MONEY

1. The student identifies the value of each coin and each bill up to twenty dollars

2. From a group of coins, picks out two different combinations that add up to 73 cents

3. In exchange for a dollar bill, gives the equivalent amount in change

4. In exchange for a ten dollar bill, gives the equivalent amount in smaller bills

5. Carries money on his person in a safe place

INDEX